FOUNDATIONS
OF ACCOUNTING

Edited by
RICHARD P. BRIEF
New York University

A GARLAND SERIES

The Auditor's Guide of 1869

■■■■■■■■■■■■■■■■■■■■■■■■■■■■■

A Review and Computer Enhancement of Recently Discovered Old Microfilm of America's First Book on Auditing by H. J. Mettenheimer

Analyzed and Restored by
PETER L. McMICKLE
PAUL H. JENSEN

GARLAND PUBLISHING, INC.
NEW YORK & LONDON 1988

For a list of Garland's publications in accounting, see the final pages of this volume.

HF
5659
M63
M38
1988

Copyright © 1988
by Peter L. McMickle and Paul H. Jensen

ROBERT MANNING
STROZIER LIBRARY

NOV 16 1989

Tallahassee, Florida

Library of Congress Cataloging-in-Publication Data

■■■■■■■■■■■■■■■■■■■■■■■■■■■■■■■■■■■

McMickle, Peter L.
The auditor's guide of 1869 : a review and computer enhanncement of recently recently by H. J. Mettenheimer / analysed and restored by Peter L. Mcmickle and Paul H. Jensen.
p. cm. —(Foundations of accounting)
Includes a photocopied reproduction of H. J. Mettenheimer's Safety book-keeping of 1875.
ISBN 0-8240-6127-6 (alk paper)
1. Mettenheimer, H. J. Auditor's guide. 2. Bookkeeping. 3. Auditing. I. Jensen, Paul H. II. Mettenheimer, H. J. Auditor's guide. 1988. III. Mettenheimer, H. J. Safety bookkeeping. 1988. IV. Title. V. Series.
HF5659.M63M38 1988
657'.45—dc19   88-17577

Design by Renata Gomes

The volumes in this series are printed on acid-free, 250-year-life paper.

Printed in the United States of America

ACKNOWLEDGEMENT

This monograph was produced in the Center of Excellence for Applied Research in Computer Applications in Accounting at the School of Accountancy, Fogelman College of Business and Economics, Memphis State University.

The publication was composed on Apple Macintosh Computers equipped with Data Frame hard disks in the Center's microcomputer lab. The manuscript was typed using Microsoft Word software. Text was then transferred to Letraset's Ready,Set,Go! 4 for editing and desktop publishing. The illustrations were digitized and enhanced using Microtek hardware and software. The final product was transmitted over an Appletalk local area network for the printing of camera-ready-copy on an Apple Laserwriter Plus.

We would particularly like to thank Richard Brief for his support and belief in this project. We are indebted to Sandra R. Banham for her excellent editorial assistance. Steve Wong's help on several aspects of the project was invaluable. Also, special thanks to a good friend and supporter, Constantine Konstans, Director of Memphis State's School of Accountancy for his strong encouragement.

Pete McMickle
Paul Jensen
April 19, 1988

TABLE OF CONTENTS

Topics	Pg.
THE LOST *AUDITOR'S GUIDE* OF 1869	3
Introduction	3
Is the *Auditor's Guide* America's First Book on Auditing?	4
Differing Views of the Objectives of Auditing	5
Description of the *Auditor's Guide* of 1869	6
A Comparative Analysis of Content Differences between the 1869 *Auditor's Guide* and the 1875 *Safety Book-keeping*	10
Conclusion	16
Restoring the *Auditor's Guide*	17
A COMPUTER RESTORATION OF H. J. METTENHEIMER'S *AUDITOR'S GUIDE* OF 1869	21
A PHOTOCOPIED REPRODUCTION OF H. J. METTENHEIMER'S *SAFETY BOOK-KEEPING* OF 1875	41

A Guide to Early American Auditing

THE LOST *AUDITOR'S GUIDE* OF 1869

Introduction

Researchers have looked to Bentley and Leonard's bibliography (1796-1934) when identifying early American works on accounting (Harry C. Bentley & Ruth S. Leonard, 1935). Their bibliography includes a classification section which lists the first American auditing book as: George Soule's *Manual of Auditing,* New Orleans, 1892 (p. 111). Additional research, published in *The Birth of American Accountancy* (McMickle and Jensen, Garland Publishing, 1988), has investigated American accounting works published prior to 1821. This study revealed no writings during the earliest period of American accountancy that pertained primarily to auditing. However, a work later than 1820 but before Soule's 1892 writing was identified.

In 1869, H. J. Mettenheimer wrote and published a book in Philadelphia entitled *Auditor's Guide Being a Complete Exposition of Bookkeeper's Frauds* (Mettenheimer, 1869). Later in 1875, he expanded the book with a new title: *Safety Book-keeping Being a Complete Exposition of Bookkeeper's Frauds* (Mettenheimer, 1875).

Although Bentley and Leonard did not list these works under auditing, they did include them in their unclassified, chronological section (p. 49). They also listed an 1877 printing but no example or evidence for this edition could be located. In addition, C. A. Moyer in a 1951 article entitled "Early Developments in American Auditing" gave a one paragraph acknowledgement of the 1869 work. He did not mention Mettenheimer's 1875 book. Despite these cites, however, the existence of Mettenhiemer's auditing work has generally gone unnoticed by contemporary accounting historians. (For example, see McMickle and Elrod, 1974, p. 10.) This is undoubtedly due in part to the exclusion of Mettenheimer from the auditing classification of Bentley and Leonard's bibliography.

The *National Union Catalog of Pre-1956 Imprints* locates only one copy of the *Auditor's Guide.* It indicates that this copy is in the Library of Congress. Five holdings of the 1875 *Safety Bookkeeping* are also shown.

Bentley and Leonard's citation for the 1869 Mettenheimer writing is identical to the one contained in the Library of Congress card catalogue in Washington. (See illustration on page 21.) It is possible that they never actually examined a copy but instead relied on Library of Congress records. Moyer does not indicate the location of the copy that he examined.

On a visit to the Library of Congress in Washington, permission to see the sole surviving copy of the *Auditor's Guide* was requested. The library representative searched for some time. Upon her return, she explained that their copy of the *Auditor's Guide* had been discarded. The representative noted that the practice was not uncommon due to the large volume of material received and subsequent warehousing problems. However, they usually microfilmed items before they were discarded and a search for a microfilm would be conducted. About a week later, a note was received that a microfilm had been located. Steps were then taken to obtain the microfilm through inter-library loan.

When the microfilm was received, only a poor, barely readable photocopy was found. From the stamp shown on the title page, it was noted that the discarded book was apparently the original copy filed for copyright by Mettenheimer in 1869. Therefore, what is apparently the first American writing on auditing is known to survive only on this single piece of microfilm.

Is the *Auditor's Guide* America's First Book on Auditing?

The 1869 *Auditor's Guide* was a paperback booklet; a mere 14 x 7.5 cm in size. It contained 14 pages of text. In the second edition entitled *Safety Book-keeping*, Mettenheimer explained that the *Auditor's Guide* "was intended as a card to introduce the author as an Auditor of Accounts. It was circulated privately and without charge." (Mettenheimer, 1875, p.v.) Despite its small size, however, the *Auditor's Guide* contained a surprising amount of technical information.

The 1875 *Safety Book-keeping* represented a major revision of the *Auditor's Guide* with much new material. It is a hardback book, 17 x 11 cm (approx. 7 x 4 1/2 inches) with 58 pages of text. In comparison, George Soule's 1892 *Manual of Auditing* is

28 x 18.5 cm with 28 pages of text. Examination reveals that the 1875 Mettenheimer text is somewhat longer than the Soule' from the standpoint of word count. However, almost half of the Soule' book (14 pages) is devoted to "Higher Accounting" topics rather than auditing, leaving only 13 pages of specific auditing material.

Thus, the 1875 *Safety Book-keeping* contains more specific material on auditing than does Soule's *Manual of Auditing*. Also, the 14 page 1869 *Auditor's Guide* contains about 60% as much auditing material as does Soule's 1892 work. Therefore, the *Auditor's Guide* certainly qualifies as a significant candidate for the first American book on auditing.

Differing Views of the Objectives of Auditing

Mettenheimer's *Auditor's Guide* of 1869 presents a different view of the objective of auditing than does Soule's 1892 *Manual of Auditing*. An early appearance of the so called modern objective of auditing is observable in Soule's *Manual of Auditing*. The focus of his auditing material is upon certification of accounts and statements.

> The Auditor should remember that, although a Financial Statement, a Trial Balance, Balance Sheet, or a Ledger may be in balance, such balance *is not proof of its correctness* ; it is only presumptive proof. Every item in a Statement of account, every debit and credit in a Trial Balance, or a Balance Sheet, and every account in a Ledger may be wrong, and yet the Statement, the Trial Balance, the Balance Sheet, or the Ledger Accounts may be in balance. Hence the Auditor must not certify Statements of Account as correct, of his own knowledge, until he has investigated them from the source to the final exhibit. These facts will not, however, prevent him, in the performance of his official duties, from accepting as correct, in many cases, various facts, figures, and accounts, on the authority of the parties whose accounts he is auditing. (Soule', 1892, p.10)

Mettenheimer's view of the objective of auditing is clearly oriented toward fraud detection as opposed to certification of the correctness of accounts and financial statements. He wrote his book with businessmen in mind as opposed to professional auditors -- who were relatively few in number at the time.

> The author has been a book-keeper for twenty years, and has been employed in auditing complicated accounts in the principal cities of the Union. He is induced to submit the results of his wide experience to the consideration of all who are compelled to entrust their books to hired or partnership assistance.
>
> That this trust is almost continually betrayed, is too well known to need comment....
>
> It is a broad assertion to make -- but a true one -- that out of the large number of books I have examined, fully one-half contained palpable evidences of fraud, and in a majority of cases where there was no previous suspicion of anything wrong. (Mettenheimer, 1875, pp. vii-8.)

Description of the *Auditor's Guide* of 1869

Mettenheimer's 14 pages of text consist of nine sections. The sections are: Auditor's Guide, Bookkeeper's Frauds, Transposition of Figures, Petty Cash Book, Bill or Note Accounts, To Prevent Fraud, Commission Purchase Account, To Prevent Fraud in the Cash Department of a Retail Store, and An Apology for Bookkeepers.

The first section referred to as "Auditor's Guide" serves as the introductory section. In this section, Mettenheimer thoroughly defends the need to investigate one's accounts, discusses the devastating extent of business frauds, touches for a moment on his own life and experience, and briefly comments on the books usefulness and style. He states that "more cases of insolvency are to be attributed to *Frauds* than shrewd businessmen are aware of" and they are urged to "give a little time to a thorough investigation of their accounts." (p. 3)

His comments on his own life include the fact that he "has been a practical bookkeeper for the past fifteen years, and has had the benefit of a wide experience." (p. 3) He continues by stating that he has been in poor health which has limited his ability to work in the "continuous sedentary confinement necessary to occupy a professional position" and offers his services as a "first class accountant, auditor, or adviser." (p. 3)

He provides numerous examples of the extent to which fraud has infiltrated the business arena and defends his opinion that all businessmen need a sufficient understanding of the methods by which accounts are investigated. The object of his "little pamphlet" is described as "to enable all concerned, whether they are conversant with the matter or not, *to audit their own accounts.*" (p. 4) He says that:

> ... you can probably save more money by spending ten minutes in reading this little book than you ever made in the same time.... So much information was never before contained in so brief a space, and so useful and sure a guide was never more needed. (pp. 3,4)

In continuing to stress the need for a sufficient understanding of auditing, Mettenheimer observes that:

> An accountant's brain is a fertile field for invention, and most of the old methods of fraud are so widely known that the imagined arbitrary remedies have become obsolete. (p. 5)

"Bookkeeper's Frauds" is the next section in *Auditor's Guide*. Mettenheimer comments that the only target of the embezzler is cash and consequently:

> ... the greater part of the trouble in detecting errors may be obviated by examining the Cash Account only.... the first thing to do is to add the long columns of the Cash Book. (p. 6)

Mettenheimer explains the best method for adding the columns and then describes the potential mistakes one can make in this addition process. The preface to the next section states that:

> Another easy plan to defraud, and one that is more frequent than the proceeding, is in the Transposition of Figures. (p. 8)

Here, Mettenheimer emphasizes that "the opportunity for doing this are legion." (p. 8) He also mentions that when an employee becomes aware of mistakes that have gone undetected by the employer, the employee becomes more prone to engage in fraudulent activities. Therefore, it is important that employers spend adequate time investigating their own accounts. He then describes how an intentional transposition error is difficult to catch because "wilful mistakes are always twins.... To discover such errors it is necessary to look over your Cash Book yourself, and to look with your eyes wide open." (p. 8)

Mettenheimer suggests that one must examine the Cash Book and Ledger for "false balancing". In this instance, the "entries and postings may all be properly made, and yet by false balancing a bookkeeper can almost defy detection in cleverly conceived and boldly executed frauds." (p. 9)

The "Petty Cash Book" section is next and "affords another opportunity for embezzlement." Mettenheimer mentions that "incorrect additions are fearfully frequent in these books." (p. 9) He also comments that:

> It is common to charge Freight Bills, Drayages, Tax Bills or other payment appertaining to Merchandise or Expense Account either twice on the same book . . . or by placing them once on the Petty Cash and once in the Cash Book. (p. 9)

Another method of obtaining cash is when a cash sale is made, the entry is posted in the Sales Book and the amount is "omitted in the monthly merchandise footing of that book." Consequently, the Sales and Petty Cash Book must be reconciled every month.

The "Bill or Note Accounts" section describes how the embezzler may obtain cash simply by charging the cash to the payment of a note payable account. Since numerous note payables are made daily, this is difficult to catch without constant scrutiny. Mettenheimer then describes how to "test the correctness of your Bills Payable account . . . and the Bills Receivable account." (p. 10) He suggests a voucher system such that the accounts be "retained, numbered and filed away as vouchers, so they can be forthcoming whenever demanded for auditing." (p. 10)

Fraud prevention is discussed in the "To Prevent Fraud" section. The author comments on the ease in which fraud can be prevented. Apathy in the maintenance of accounts, for whatever reason, is a primary problem in fraud occurrence. Mettenheimer provides suggestions for reducing fraud.

First – "Order is Heaven's first law" and therefore, "all entries. . . should be clear, full, and explicit. . ." (p. 11)

Second – "have numerical lines ruled in the money columns of your books; for any accountant can render your attempt to investigate the integrity of his arithmetic almost an impossibility by slovenly numeration. . ." (p. 12)

Third – "Audit your own Cash Book during the dull season of every year." (p. 12) Mettenheimer then describes a short system for auditing your own cash book.

Fourth – "Keep an exact duplicate of the Petty Cash book yourself. . . ." (p. 12)

Fifth – "Have every item composing a Bank Deposit entered in detail on the margin of your Check book. This will serve to settle any difference of opinion existing between your customers and your bookkeepers in regard to alleged payments. . . ." (p. 13)

Sixth – "Be honest with yourself, and do not stoop to small swindles for trifling gains." (p. 13) The author emphasizes this by stating that "bookkeepers will remember these things . . . for the purpose of a countercharge in case of threatened prosecution for fraud." (p. 13)

Seventh – "Pay the man who takes care of your money a salary sufficient for his family support." (p. 13) Apparently, the bookkeeper is not apt to embezzle if an adequate salary is provided. The author finishes this section by stating that "the laborer is worthy of his hire; and if he don't get it in one way, he will in another." (p. 13)

In the "Commission Purchase Account" section, the author describes how the commission merchants have an incentive to embezzle through the subsidiary purchase ledger they maintain. He states that "as keeping this account offers considerable incentive to fraud, it should be audited several times a year." (p. 14) Mettenheimer emphasizes that one should "make it a practice to thoroughly check this and every other *Labor Saving Account* as often as convenient." (p. 15)

The author, in an effort to make the book "more complete", provides the "To Prevent Fraud in the Cash Department of a Retail Store" section. Mettenheimer comments that "many storekeepers have been utterly ruined by their Cashiers. . . ." (p. 15) He then offers a "safe and simple method" for checking a day's cash sales. The method revolves around a duplicate sales ticket in which one is given to the Cashier and the other dropped in a locked box.

The book ends with a section entitled "An Apology for Bookkeepers." The author begins this section with the comment that "if there exists any excuse for fraud, bookkeepers are entitled to it." (p. 16)   He observes that the bookkeeper generally is poorly paid, observes contradictory behavior by the employer, and concludes that embezzlement is justified. "He sees his principal preach honesty and practice fraud . . . and concludes that it is easier to steal money that to earn it." (p. 16) Mettenheimer ends the book by suggesting that if employers wants cheap assistance:

> . . . they should learn that the counting room is not the department to save in. Let them give their bookkeepers a better prospect than a pauper's grave, and they will have less reason to apprehend fraud. (p. 16)

A Comparative Analysis of Content Differences between the 1869 *Auditor's Guide* and the 1875 *Safety Book-keeping*

Content Unique to the 1869 *Auditor's Guide*

Most of the text found in the *Auditor's Guide* is also contained in the 1875 *Safety Book-keeping*. Only a few words or phrases are eliminated in the *Safety Book-keeping* edition.

Mettenheimer stated in his introduction that he "had been a practical bookkeeper for the past fifteen years, and has had the benefit of a wide experience, to which his list of references will attest." He also identified one of the reasons he was offering his services as a public auditor by stating, in the third person, that:

> . . . increasing ill health has debarred him from the continuous sedentary continement necessary to occupy a professional position, and he therefore offers his services to parties who require the temporary aid of a first-class accountant, auditor, or advisor. (p. 3)

Mettenheimer's *Auditor's Guide* also contained a section referred to as the "Commission Purchase Account" which was later completely rewritten, retitled, and expanded into a section in *Safety Book-keeping* entitled "City invoice-books."

Content Unique to the 1875 *Safety Book-keeping*

In the "Preface to the Present Edition," Mettenheimer expounds upon his intentions of distributing the first book and clarifies his reasons for this new edition. He states that the first edition was circulated privately and without charge. He also mentions that there were some objections to the indiscriminate distribution, because:

> 'If the work falls into the hands of book-keepers, it might teach them something of which they are ignorant, and impel them to do just what it is intended to prevent.'
> (p. v)

He refutes this concern by stating that:

> ... a man who is dishonest can always conceive methods of his own for committing crime without instruction, and a necessity therefore arises for Employers to be informed of such conceptions, and provided with the means of preventing their execution. (p. v)

Mettenheimer continues by stating that:

> The author therefore contends that his book will deter more than it will ever incite to wrong-doing. (p. v)

Also contained in this new section is a description of the design of the second edition and a listing of the major firms for which he performed accounting services. The design of his book is to "point out where trouble in accounts arise; to show how they may be obviated; and to prevent its readers from becoming victims to fraud." (p. vi) He concludes this section with a listing of the firms by which he has been employed from the periods 1855 - 1875. He states that "he has also adjusted complicated accounts for other business houses from New York to Texas." (p. vi)

Mettenheimer extensively expanded the "Introduction" section. Found within this added text is the statement that many merchants lack only one qualification to conduct a business successfully, and this encompasses an "ignorance of a method to govern their accounts." (p. vii) Another interesting addition is the mention that "the most stupendous defalcations are perpetrated by *partners* who have acted as cashiers. What is called embezzlement in an employee, is known as a breach of trust when committed by a partner, and as such, is exempt from criminal prosecution." (p. 8)

In the "Book-keeper's Fraud" section, he provides only one addition which is a small paragraph explaining the inability to depend upon the Trial Balance. He states that a "Trial Balance taken from a defaulter's work proves nothing, unless it be a little expertness on the part of the operator in concealing intentional error." (p. 12)

In the *Auditor's Guide*, Mettenheimer described transposition of errors in a paragraph format. In the expanded "Transposition of Figures" section, he reorganizes this explanation into a columnar format which is much easier to visualize. He also talks of the potential magnitude of the errors and how the amount may simply depend upon the bookkeepers attitude and that it may occur "as often as your book-keeper considers it consistent with his own ideas of propriety." He gives an example of this:

> One instance came under my own observation in Philadelphia, where it appeared as if the *partner* who was *running the cash*, really thought he would do himself an injustice by making a correct entry. (p. 18)

"Original Ledger Entries and False Ledger Balances" is a completely new section found in this edition. The section deals with deliberate or *careless* delinquency in recording cash receipts. Mettenheimer suggests that this is an extremely difficult fraud to find and that:

> To discover the aggregate of such embezzlements, it is necessary to test the virtue of every balance on your Ledger, and to examine every entry, footing, posting, and balance that has any connection with your 'Merchandise account' on every book in use. (p. 19)

He says that he "would not therefore recommend a search requiring so much labor, unless you are convinced that you are harboring a scamp in your counting-room, and are anxious to fasten some act upon him." (p. 20)

The "Petty Cash-Books" section is significantly expanded including some columnar format examples. He describes the cash books and then supplies a couple of examples of recording cash transactions. Mettenheimer describes how little attention is paid to these books and that they "when filled up, are frequently lost sight of entirely." (p. 23)

The "Bill or Note Accounts" section is also considerably increased including the addition of examples of the Bills Receivable and Bills Payable general ledger accounts. The *Linear System* is described as the "safest, best, and most convenient way of keeping Note Accounts." (p. 25)   He continues the description stating:

> By this method each note is posted on a separate line in the Ledger page, and whenever one is paid, the payment is posted on the contra side of the same line. Then, when you wish to know the number and amount of those unpaid, you have only to count the unbalanced spaces. By this method. . . no difficulty is occasioned in discovering at a glance how much is due you, and by whom. . .
> (pp. 25, 26)

In the section entitled "City Invoice-Books", Mettenheimer completely revises the "Commission Purchase Account" contained in the *Auditor's Guide.*   He explains that general business concerns will buy just enough merchandise from specialty merchandisers to fill their daily orders and therefore:

> . . . an immense number of small bills are accumulated during a month. To avoid filling a Ledger too rapidly with these trifling postings, the City Invoice-book was adopted, the purpose being to aggregate at the end of the month all bills purchased from each particular house, and post it *en masse* to the credit of that house. (p. 27)

However, Mettenheimer observes that the use of the city invoice account system "offers such brilliant opportunities for theft, as to warrant either its discontinuance or a decided limitation of its use." (p. 27)

In the "Commissions Purchase Account" section of the *Auditor's Guide* , he merely notes that the account should be audited several times a year if possible. The "Short Cash" section is entirely new and came about as a result of a fraudulent act brought to Mettenheimer's attention. The act consisted of a cashier gradually stealing money and concealing the shortage by delaying the recording of customer payments. Mettenheimer states that the:

> . . . concealment for so long a time was only made possible by the extreme confidence that had been reposed in the defaulter by his principals. No fraudulent entries had been made to cover the deficiency, and it was only discovered upon a dissolution of partnership. (p. 29)

The fraudulent technique described by Mettenheimer is similar to what is currently called "lapping" in which the receipt of cash for one account is used to cover the delinquency of another as a result of a theft.

In the new "Book-keeper's Personal Account" the business owner is cautioned about allowing the bookkeeper to maintain a personal account on the owner's ledger. Mettenheimer explains that:

> In investigating suspicious accounts, it is frequently discovered that book-keepers have taken money from the Cash Drawer, charged it to themselves (probably before their employer's eyes), and then deliberately posted the item to 'Merchandise' or 'Expense.' (p. 31)

He talks about identifying a thief by occasionally inquiring:

> ... into your book-keeper's style of living, and see if it corresponds with the salary he is getting . . . a visit to his place of residence might throw considerable light on how much it would require to maintain his establishment. While anything like a sneaking surveillance is to be condemned, a little sociability with an employee, in order to learn his habits, is certainly to be commended in an employer. (pp. 31,32)

"Pay-Rolls" is the next section which is unique to *Safety Book-keeping*. In this section Mettenheimer cautions the owner about allowing a larger number of employees to purchase supplies or other items against their own personal accounts. He suggests maintaining a separate account in the Ledger entitled "Payroll". He provides a rather detailed description of payroll transactions including a half page of journal entries. He mentions that two signatures would be helpful but not infallible by stating that:

> It would do no harm to require the signatures of both the journeyman, clerk, or laborer getting the money, and of the department manager or section 'boss' on the line representing each particular payment, but this would not be an infallible remedy where a determination to steal existed. (p. 35)

The "Gold Bills" section is also unique to *Safety Bookkeeping*. Mettenheimer says that:

Importers and dealers in foreign merchandise are in the habit of charging goods to their customers at so much in gold. This is rendered necessary on account of the fluctuation that may take place in the price of gold between the date of sale and the date of payment. The first debit is at a gold price, and when the bill is paid, a second debit should be made. (p. 36)

He goes on to say that:

A book-keeper is here afforded an opportunity to absorb the amount of the premium by omitting the latter ceremony altogether, and as there is no charge to any personal account for the premium, the matter is not likely to be discovered. (p. 36)

Bad debts are discussed in the new "Collection Account" section. He suggests that rather than charging the bad debts to "Profit and Loss", a separate "Collection Account" should be used. He provides a General Ledger example of the Collection Account. He says that separate accounts for uncollectibles are "scattered all over the ledger." (p. 38) He then suggests a new approach by stating that:

... it is easier to watch such accounts under *one head* than under a different head for each different note or account. I would therefore suggest that you purge the different pages of your Ledger of such claims as are already in litigation, and bring them together under a new head, called 'Collection Account'. (pp. 38-39)

"A Well-Known Fraud" is another totally new section in which Mettenheimer describes a specific fraudulent attempt by bookkeepers. It pertains to a situation where the bookkeeper receives cash and yet records the receipt in the Merchandise account rather than the cash account.

An account similar to a Petty Cash account is introduced in the "Salary Signature-Book" section. It is recommended that personal withdrawals be maintained separately in a "Salary Signature-book" and the total posted only at the end of month.

"To Prevent Fraud in the Cash Department of Retail Stores" is a section that is modified from the 1869 *Auditor's Guide*. Mettenheimer provides for internal cash control by recommending that "the Cash Drawer should be handled by one person only. Not even the head of a firm should be allowed a key to it." (p. 45) He discusses the need for prenumbered sales slips with three copies. One goes to the cashier, one to the salesman and one is dropped in a locked box for recording at a later date.

The "To Prevent Fraud" section has only minor modifications from the *Auditor's Guide*. In this section, Mettenheimer states that "the popular system of posting several entries in one should never be permitted." (p. 50) He also describes the method to verify the "Balance on Hand" by analyzing the "bank-book balanced in bank, and the sum there left to your credit, together with what is in the Cash Drawer." (p. 51)

Mettenheimer concludes the *Safety Book-keeping* text with two totally new sections entitled "Remedies at Law for Frauds in Book-keeping" and "a Check on Hazardous Credits." In the former section he mentions that "the law affords parties who have been victimized by fraudulent book-keeping very little chance for redress." (p. 57) He continues by discussing various legal cases and describes some of the difficulties encountered in successfully bringing cases to trial.

In the later section, Mettenheimer introduces a new concept for minimizing the risk of delinquent accounts. He purposes the now widely used concept of credit bureaus. He suggests that a new office should be established in the business center of the city. The new office would contain accounts of all the delinquent customers in the city. Businesses would bring each delinquent account to the new office, and a separate page would be entered by each customer. Each morning, the new office would be informed of payments received and the delinquent accounts would be adjusted. He states that:

> A complete record can thus be kept of the entire amount of indebtedness of every person buying goods in the city. (p. 62)

Conclusion

Unfortunately, almost nothing is known about the author, H. J. Mettenheimer, outside of the comments about himself contained in his books. The *National Union Catalogue of Pre-1956 Imprints* does identify two four act plays published by Mettenheimer in addition to his work on auditing.

Other contenders for the title of the first American auditing book could well emerge. However, it seems apparent that the *Auditor's Guide* and *Safety Book-keeping* are significant historical works that provide an important perspective of the nature of mid-nineteenth century American auditing.

Restoring the *Auditor's Guide*

The reproduction of the *Auditor's Guide* that begins on page 23 is the result of a computerized restoration effort. The Library of Congress made a microfilm copy of the *Auditor's Guide* before they discarded it. However, this copy is reduced much more than today's normal 35mm microfilmed record, and it is out of focus with many surface scratches and other mars. A positive copy of the film was found to be of poor quality and difficult to read.

A variety of different brands of microfilm copiers were tried in an attempt to obtain a positive copy good enough to use as a start for the restoration process. All of these trial copies proved to be unsatisfactory. The microfilm was then taken to a commercial photography lab and the positive used for the restoration was obtained with a photo-enlarger shooting on fine grained, high gloss photograph paper.

The photographs were then used to create computer graphic files. This was done by scanning the photos with a Microtek MS-300A intelligent image scanner connected to an Apple Macintosh Plus and a Dataframe 20 megabyte hard disk. The Macintosh had been upgraded for graphics use by increasing the RAM memory to 2.5 megabytes. The software used to drive the scanning process and perform the restoration was Microtek's VersaScan+ 1.01. Each page resulted in a file that averaged around 700K bytes. The total 17 pages of the book accounted for 11.8 megabytes of hard disk space.

The pages were enhanced on the computer screen by using a mouse pointing device to restore the images on a pixel by pixel basis. The graphics were then directly typeset within the same computer environment using Letraset's Ready,Set,Go! 4.0. The final product was sent over an Appletalk local area network to an Apple Laserwriter Plus printer. The 17 pages took over four hours to print.

REFERENCES

Bentley, H. C. and R. S. Leonard. *Bibliography of Works on Accounting by American Authors.* 2 Vols. Boston: Harry C. Bentley, 1934, 1935.

Mettenheimer, H. J, *Auditor's Guide Being a Complete Exposition of Bookkeeper's Fraud.* Philadelphia: H. J. Mettenheimer, 1869.

_____. *Safety Book-keeping.* Cincinnati: Robert Clarke & Co., 1875.

Moyer, C. A. "Early Developments in American Auditing," *The Accounting Review,* XXVI, (January, 1951).

Soule', George. *Manual of Auditing.* 1st edition. New Orleans: George Soule', 1892.

The National Union Catalog: Pre-1956 Imprints. 700 Vols. London: Mansell Information/Publishing Limited and The American Library Association, 1971.

A COMPUTER RESTORATION

OF

H. J. METTENHEIMER'S

AUDITOR'S GUIDE

OF

1869

COMPUTER ENHANCED FROM THE SURVIVING MICROFILM OF
THE BOOK SUBMITTED FOR COPYRIGHT PROTECTION BY THE
AUTHOR TO THE LIBRARY OF CONGRESS

THE COPY SIZE HAS BEEN ENLARGED FOR READABILITY
FROM THE ORIGINAL 14 x 7.5 CM

56533

Mettenheimer, H   J.
   Auditor's guide; being a complete exposition of book-
keeper's frauds ... Also containing a new and safe method
of managing the cash department of retail stores, and a
purchase account for commission houses ... [By] H. J.
Mettenheimer.   Philadelphia, The author [¹1869]
   16 p. 14ᶜᵐ.

1. Bookkeeping. 2. Auditing.

Library of Congress   HF5659.M6   CA 8—3291 Unrev'd
                            [s20b1]

The Library of Congress catalogue card for Mettenheimer's *Auditor's Guide*, shown above after restoration, was photographed as the first frame of the archived microfilm record.

AUDITOR'S GUIDE

BEING A COMPLETE EXPOSITION OF

BOOKKEEPER'S FRAUDS.

How Committed!

How Concealed!

How Discovered!

How Prevented!

Also containing a new and safe method of managing the

CASH DEPARTMENT OF RETAIL STORES,

AND A

PURCHASE ACCOUNT FOR COMMISSION HOUSES.

The design of this book is to point out where trouble in accounts arise; to show how they may be obviated; and so prevent my readers becoming victims of fraud in the future.

Published and Sold only by the Author,

H. J. METTENHEIMER,

114 South Sixth Street,

ROOM No. 7, LEDGER BUILDING.   PHILADELPHIA.

HF5659
.M6

Entered according to Act of Congress in the year 1869, by
H. J. METTENHEIMER,
In the Clerk's office of the District Court of the Eastern
District of Pennsylvania.

AUDITOR'S GUIDE.

As you can probably save more money by spending ten minutes in reading this little book than you ever made in the same time, your careful attention is directed to the following:

Many men, wise in their own conceit, suffer loss and bankruptcy and never know the cause. More cases of insolvency are to be attributed to *Frauds* than shrewd business men are aware of, and though the advice is almost universally unpopular, it is urged on merchants to overcome their disinclination for this species of labor, and give a little time to a thorough investigation of their accounts. The author has been a practical bookkeeper for the past fifteen years, and has had the benefit of a wide experience, to which his list of references will attest. Increasing ill health has debarred him from the continuous sedentary confinement necessary to occupy a professional position, and he therefore offers his services to parties who require the temporary aid of a first-class accountant, auditor, or adviser.

Having been employed in auditing complicated accounts in the principal cities of the Union, he has determined to reap the benefit of the experience thus acquired, and is induced to submit this little compendium to the consideration of all who are compelled to entrust their books to hired assistance.

That this trust is almost continually betrayed by employees is too well known to need comment. Newspapers daily chronicle the detection of new cases of embezzlement, and still our merchants shut their eyes and believe all servants dishonest but their own. While they admit the shrewdness of their accountants in other matters, they blindly imagine them too trustworthy, or too fearful of consequences to deceive them in regard to the manipulation of their finances; yet in case of the death of an old favorite bookkeeper, or even of a partner, who has had the management of the cash, how often do we find that their apparently beautifully balanced accounts are teeming with a succession of fraudulent entries that had been continued through years.

Published defalcations are but a small fraction of the number really committed. Confidential relations existing between bookkeepers and one or more of their employers, are the causes why so few embezzlement cases come to light. Most houses have secrets that they do not wish exposed, and in addition to having their own credit impaired by prosecuting a defaulter, they would have their weak places divulged in retaliation; hence, a great preponderance of frauds are always privately compromised.

You will acknowledge the truth of these statements, and say you are powerless to apply a remedy; that your manifold duties prevent you from attending to your counting-room; that you are ignorant of the technicalities of bookkeeping and cannot discover errors even if so disposed. The object of this little pamphlet is to enable all concerned, whether they are conversant with the matter or not, *to audit their own accounts*.

The style is plain, the matter condensed, and the subject exhausted in these few pages. So much information was never before contained in so brief a space, and so useful and sure a guide was never more needed. After reading it, you may think the suggestions very appropriate, but imagine you cannot spare the time to heed them. This is the rock on which many a proud commercial craft has gone to pieces, and on which you may swamp at any moment. It is therefore urged on you to try to give the matter your personal attention, and what has heretofore seemed a tangled labyrinth, will after a little practice become as clear and practicable as the noon-day sun. Nothing is easier to comprehend and master than a distasteful medley of figures after a few days trial. By spending a few moments each day over your books, you will be surprised how quickly you can accomplish what had hitherto occupied so long a time, and if you will reflect that your safety, your fortune, and your ultimate happiness almost entirely depend on your own care and scrutiny, you will no longer hesitate to overcome a personal dislike for the details of accounts that is almost universal.

Perhaps the safest prey for skilful bookkeepers are parties who believe they are too proficient in the science to be swindled. The fault here is, that while a rogue will avoid a breaker known to all, and conform to such established forms as some employers prescribe as an absolute check to fraud, he will be operating in a channel of which his employer is ignorant. An accountant's brain is a fertile field for invention, and most of the old methods of fraud are so widely known that the imagined arbitrary remedies have become obsolete, except in the minds of employers, who consider themselves beyond learning anything new. To such this little work is especially recommended, though it is doubtful whether they will not continue in the belief of their own infallibility.

"It is better to do one thing well than attempt to do more and only half do them." One business is enough for most mortals, and if you care for your legitimate occupation, it don't pay to trust it to subordinates, and employ your own time in outside speculations. Employees know full well when their principals are too much engaged in other pursuits to watch their actions very closely, and their assumed devotion to the interests of their employers is only a cloak to cover their own rascality. If you can make one thousand dollars by kite-flying, while a clerk is stealing five thousand that might have been saved by your own vigilance, you are a heavy loser in the end, and will only probably learn better when too late. Admitting the worldly inhumanity of the advice to *trust no man*, it is well known that the most successful merchants are those who adopt so harsh and uncharitable a rule.

BOOKKEEPER'S FRAUDS.

As the only benefit to be derived from frauds in accounts arises from a desire to embezzle the *cash*, the greater part of the trouble in detecting errors may be obviated by examining the Cash Account only. Fully three-fourths of the remaining labor may be avoided by testing the additions, as a defrauder is in most cases particularly careful to make his original entries correctly. Strange as it may appear to a novice in auditing, it seldom pays to examine if the proper credits are given for cash payments, because errors of this kind are so liable to accidental detection that a first-class rogue would not attempt to make them.

In the additions or manipulation of the figures alone need employers hope to readily discover how they are swindled, and the first thing to do is to add the long columns of the Cash Book. Do this thoroughly, and if you fail to find the addition of the debit side, $10, $100, or $1,000, too little, or the credit side $10, $100, or $1,000 too great, you can resort to our next plan.

You may argue that a bookkeeper would not dare do this because the discrepancy would appear in the Trial Balance. He can cover his tracks very easily, however, by making a corresponding error in the footings of the Journal, and if you examine your merchandise, expense, or any but a personal account, you will find a mistake on the contra side for the deficit in cash. Of course, two errors of the same amount, but on different sides, will result in a balance of the books. These forced balances and double mistakes are always intentional and never occur by accident.

As but few persons are expert in adding, the following plan may be of service to parties who are not skilful at the work. Run your columns both up and down, so one may prove the other. In casting up a page, place the total of first column down in pencil; carry all but the right hand figure to the next column, and place the result of this column under the other, carrying all but the right hand figure to the next column, and so on until the page is complete. The entire figures of the last footing and the units of the others will be the total of the page, thus:

```
18294.12
19183.01
27696.20
39172.21
18096.12
27171.03
19096.11
28184.00
19075.20
38196.13
29082.01
18198.14
29073.20
16299.10
57182.31
29396.12
49183.24
38692.33    5-3 first column.
28394.06    3-4 second  "
49088.27    11-4 third  "
38394.26    21-1 fourth "
59287.15    5-1 fifth   "
29184.01    20-3 sixth  "
18096.10    74 seventh  "
Total....743114.43    743114.43
```

In a hasty addition of the foregoing, you are liable to the following errors:

In the *third* column by carrying *one* instead of *eleven;* in the *fourth* column by carrying *eleven* instead of *twenty-one;* in the *fifth* column by carrying *fifteen* instead of *five;* and in the *sixth* column by carrying *ten* instead of *twenty.*

Try this, and see how easy it is to get the total down wrong. Every one but experienced accountants frequently fail to carry enough figures after they reach one hundred, and it is right here where the bookkeeper knows and possesses his advantage to make ten, one hundred, or one thousand dollars occasionally.

We would suggest that you require all cash footings pencilled and left standing as in the example, and if your cashier is honest, he will not object to comply with the requirement.

Another easy plan to defraud, and one that is more frequent than the preceding, is in the

TRANSPOSITION OF FIGURES.

The opportunities for doing this are legion, and as every occurrence of the kind may be covered in the Trial Balance by a corresponding transposition in some representative account as before, of course the much vaunted Trial Balance Sheet does not prove the correctness of the books.

It sometimes happens that figures are transposed by accident, but when this is the case, the accounts will fail to accord until the error is discovered and corrected. An accountant perceiving that an accidental fault has remained undetected for a long time by his employers, and then only found out by himself, becomes more venturesome thereafter, repeating the thing wilfully and with intent to defraud. In the first instance there is no contra error, but wilful mistakes are always twins.

Suppose your cashier receives $2,979, and credits it on the cash book $2,799, making $180 for himself; or, suppose he pays $33,533, and charges it $35,333, and puts $1,800 in his pocket; what employer would be apt to notice it? Here the original entry can be made wrong, while the right figures may be posted, and the discrepancy balanced or counteracted in merchandise or some other such account. Experienced detectives have checked through a set of books, passing over instances of this apparently impossible chance for fraud, just because the figures looked and sounded as if they were correct.

Again, if in footing a page of the cash book, the debtor side foots $19,789, and is carried forward $17,989, or the credit side foots $17,989, and is carried forward $19,789, it is palpable that the cashier has made a clean sweep of $1,800 outside of his salary.

To discover such errors it is necessary to look over your Cash Book yourself, and to look with your eyes wide open. It is surprising how often you may look at a mistake of this kind, and yet fail to detect it. Also examine if so-called *balances* are correct both on the Cash Book when apparently balanced, and occasionally try the virtue of balances that appear on the Ledger in both personal and representative accounts. Entries and postings may all be properly made, and yet by false balancing a bookkeeper can almost defy detection in cleverly conceived and boldly executed frauds.

PETTY CASH BOOKS.

These afford another opportunity for embezzlement. It is common to charge Freight Bills, Drayages, Tax Bills or other payments appertaining to Merchandise or Expense Account either twice on the same book, by entering one separately and the same one in connection with others paid on the same day, or by placing them once on the Petty Cash and once in the large Cash Book. When a bill is paid by a customer before the entry is posted from the Sales Book, it is customary to mark the same paid, and the amount omitted in the monthly merchandise footing of that book. This is very correct provided the payment is entered as a cash sale on the Petty Cash Book, and you should see that this is never forgotten. The date of liquidation should be placed on the Sales Book when the amount is marked paid, and you had better compare these marks with the Petty Cash Book every month, and see that cash has been debited with the money in every instance.

Incorrect additions are fearfully frequent in these books, and as they are seldom inspected, the cashier, if he apprehends they will be looked over at some future time, can and does make false entries to balance the wrong additions. This is done after a sufficient time has elapsed for an employer to forget the probable circumstances of such payments as are inserted being made, and of course this tampering would then escape his scrutiny.

BILL OR NOTE ACCOUNTS.

Some concerns doing a very heavy note business, never think of going any further than striking a balance on these accounts when they wish to ascertain the amount of notes due them, or how much they owe in outstanding paper of their own. If their books are kept correctly, this balance of course will give them the information desired, but it is just as often that false entries have been made here as elsewhere. If you are in the habit of giving a note for every bill purchased from houses with whom you deal often, your cashier may have a habit of charging cash with a note every now and then that you have never given and which never existed. Even if you daily examine your Cash Book you will not be apt to look too closely at an entry "By Bills Payable, paid John Jones' note due this day," when similar entries are of almost daily occurrence. You will naturally take it for granted that this note is one of the many you have given John Jones, when perhaps if you refer to your Note Book you will discover that there was none due on this day, and that the amount so charged is a fraud.

To test the correctness of your Bills Payable account, you should add the amount of notes remaining unpaid on the Note Book, and this must agree with the credit balance of your Bills Payable account on the Ledger. When *paid*, all notes should be retained, and numbered and filed away as vouchers in the same manner as ordinary receipts, so they can be forthcoming whenever demanded for auditing.

To test the correctness of your Bills Receivable account, the amount of all notes or acceptances you hold in your possession should agree with the debit balance of the Bills Receivable account on the Ledger.

In investigating suspicious accounts, we have frequently discovered that bookkeepers have taken money from the Cash Drawer, charged it to themselves, (probably before their employer's eyes,) and then deliberately posted the item to Merchandize or Expense. Hence, it might pay to see if your Cashier's monetary supplies always appear to his debit on the Ledger.

TO PREVENT FRAUD.

It is so easy a thing to prevent fraudulent bookkeeping that it is really surprising to find so many merchants become the victims to this species of dishonesty. All men of good commercial capacity find it necessary to reduce the different departments of their business to a system, and, as a general thing, require a strict observance of their regulations from their employees. The one exception to this vigilance seems to be exactly where such vigilance is most required; and the apathy of business classes to the subject of their accounts is the more singular, from the fact that correct records are of the utmost importance to a knowledge of their own solvency. This apathy cannot arise from indifference to office affairs, or it would prove a penny-wise and pound-foolish management that merchants do not possess. It is either ignorance of bookkeeping, or a modest disinclination to interfere in the irksome details of the desk, that cause first-class business men to lose money, while their Cashiers are growing rich.

By requiring a strict adherence to the following suggestions from the occupants of their counting-rooms, principals can thoroughly close up all the channels of fraud, and we are satisfied a little reflection will cause their universal adoption.

First. Order is Heaven's first law, and the science of accounts is founded on this law. Books of account are or should be a history of all transactions relating directly or indirectly to your finances. To record the events of this history in a careful manner, so you will remember the circumstance at any time in the future, is one object in keeping commercial books. All entries, therefore, should be clear, full, and explicit; much verbiage is unnecessary, but enough should be stated to render each record incapable of perversion or misconstruction. If you merely enter "Bills Payable, Dr., To Cash, $5,000," and post it without further explanation, you cannot tell in a year after the entry is made whose note was paid without referring to your note book; but if you only subjoin "For John Smith's note, maturing this day," you can turn to the original entry made when the note was given, and learn what you are paying your $5,000 for. Without some such short statement following each entry, your bookkeeper might give you any answer to inquiries about suspicious matters that best suited the description of fraud he was attempting to cover.

Second. Have numerical lines ruled in the money columns of your books; for any accountant can render your attempt to investigate the integrity of his arithmetic almost an impossibility by slovenly numeration; placing units under tens, tens under hundreds, and hundreds under thousands. Apparent carelessness in this particular is frequently designed rascality.

Third. Audit your own Cash book during the dull season every year. This seems like a very heavy undertaking, and from which most persons will recoil at the first impulse. It can be simplified, however, so as to make it rather an easy and pleasant summer recreation. For every payment that is made, a receipt or voucher should be taken. Make this an absolute duty with your Cashier. This voucher should be numbered, and a corresponding number placed on the entry relating to it. The vouchers should be filed carefully away in their proper order, and when the time is at hand for auditing, every voucher should be forthcoming. The work of comparing can then be accomplished very rapidly, and a few days will suffice to check up the entire cash business of a year. By a little practice in our rules for addition previously given, you can soon become sufficiently expert in adding a column to go through every page of your Cash Book in a day or two more. When you reflect how this course may save you as much as the rest of your year's profits, we think the junior partners of large business houses will not hesitate a moment to utilize our plan.

Fourth. Keep an exact duplicate of the Petty Cash book yourself; that is, have a book exactly like it, and take a copy every night of the daily items and footings from the one in your bookkeeper's possession. This certainly will not occupy more than five minutes daily, and it is an effectual check against backward tampering.

Fifth. Have every item composing a Bank Deposit entered in detail on the margin of your Check book. This will serve to settle any difference of opinion existing between your customers and your bookkeepers in regard to alleged payments of which your books contain no record. If an amount, corresponding to a payment claimed to be made, appears on the margin on the date it is said to have been made, the evidence against your Cashier is clear. If no such amount is to be found, you will be warranted in insisting on a re-payment.

Sixth. Be honest yourself and do not stoop to small swindles for trifling gains. Never use revenue stamps twice, and never keep money received by error in counting. Bookkeepers remember these things, and treasure the recollection for the purpose of a countercharge in case of threatened prosecution for fraud.

Seventh. Pay the man who takes care of your money a salary sufficient for his family support. If you hear of any Real Estate purchases, or other speculations of your bookkeeper, it would profit you to ascertain how and where he derives the money to operate with. If you suspect that your own Cash Drawer is the source, or that your money is maintaining an extravagant expenditure not commensurate with the salary you are paying, you had better discharge the man, and hire one who can live within the amount you are willing to allow him. If your business profits are too small to meet the demands of a competent and trustworthy assistant, you will find it to your interest to do your own work. "The laborer is worthy of his hire;" and if he don't get it in one way, he will in another.

COMMISSION PURCHASE ACCOUNT.

Commission merchants are continually entrusted with orders from their customers for the purchase of a great variety of merchandise out of their regular line.

To obviate the necessity of opening accounts with each concern for whom or from whom these purchases are made, it is customary to keep a small auxiliary Ledger by single entry; otherwise, the main Ledger would soon become filled with the names of a legion of parties whose limited transactions would hardly warrant giving them such prominence.

On this Purchase Ledger, parties for whom purchases are made are debited with the amount of each bill purchased for their account, together with charges for Commissions, Insurance, Freight, Cartages, &c. Parties from whom purchases are made are credited with the amount of their bills rendered, less the commission they allow for the patronage bestowed.

A Purchase Account is opened on the main Ledger; and where remittances are received, this account is credited on the Cash Book: "To Purchase Account, received from * * *," and the remitted sums removed from the Purchase Book. When bills rendered by others are paid, cash is credited: "By Purchase Account, paid * * *," and the party to whom such payment is made has his account balanced from the Purchase Book. Once a month, the total amount of all commissions, and the profit on Insurance, Freight, and Cartage, should be collected from this Purchase Book, and placed to the credit of Purchase Account on the main Ledger. This ought to produce a credit balance to represent the profit for the work and labor bestowed on this branch of the Commission business, and merchants are frequently amazed at the scanty exhibit of profit it presents.

As keeping this account offers considerable incentive to fraud, it should be audited several times a year. Perhaps in checking your Cash Book, it will be found that Freights, Cartages, and Insurance, have been overcharged; or the same bills may have been charged twice; or entries may have been made for bills that were never incurred, and of course never paid; or double entries made for the same payment against your regular business, and also against this Purchase Account.

Always make it a practice to thoroughly check this and every other *Labor Saving Account* as often as convenient; for even though a profitable exhibit is presented, it is easy to give them this appearance by false accumulations of Commissions.

TO PREVENT FRAUD IN THE CASH DEPARTMENT OF A RETAIL STORE.

To render our little work more complete, a suggestion for the benefit of Retail Dealers may not be inappropriate.

Many storekeepers have been utterly ruined by their Cashiers, even while the establishments enjoyed a good run of custom and the business was otherwise conducted on paying principles. Quite a number of plans for checking and counter-checking a day's cash sales have been devised, and without commenting on them all, we would recommend the following safe and simple method as the best.

The Cash Drawer should be handled by one person only. Every time a clerk makes a sale, he should place the amount on *two* tickets, affixing his name or initials to each. One of these should be given to the Cashier, with the money, and the other dropped into a slit cut in a locked box, the key of which should be kept by the proprietor. The duplicate blanks can be furnished to the clerks on one slip of paper, each half containing a corresponding number; and when used, should be torn in half, one piece going to the Cashier, the other to the locked box.

The merit of this plan is, that everything is completed on the spur of the moment; and the fact of one ticket having gone beyond the reach of being destroyed or tampered with, the possibility of Cashier and Salesman conniving to alter figures at their leisure during the day is prevented.

Of course, the amount of the day's sales ought to equal the sum of the tickets in the box, which should be counted nightly by the proprietor.

Under the old individual pass or sales-book system an employer is so often cheated by reputed errors in sales, when evidences of alteration occur too often, that we think it best for him to attend to such changes himself, even if our method is adopted. In cases of error, or of money refunded for goods returned, we would advise that all such claims be submitted to one of the heads of the establishment, who alone should place in the duplicate ticket box all slips referring to drawbacks.

The clerk's entry books, however, can be used in connection with our plan, if preferred.

AN APOLOGY FOR BOOKKEEPERS.

If there exists any excuse for fraud, bookkeepers are entitled to it.

As a general thing, the profession is too poorly paid, considering the sacrifice of health, the necessity of maintaining a gentlemanly appearance, and the poor prospect of advancement. To do his whole duty, a bookkeeper is obliged to confine himself to the distasteful monotony of his employment in a manner that will speedily convert him into a mechanical overworked drone. He sees his principal preach honesty and practice fraud; and perceiving that dishonesty prospers in spite of the frightful stories to the contrary, concludes that it is easier to steal money than to earn it. He soon learns that where one swindle is published a hundred remain undiscovered, and so is led to appropriate whatever he can to his own use. He knows that if a stone is thrown at him, he can throw a heavier one back; and if his employers are too blind to place his salary at a deserving figure, he considers himself justifiable for secretly supplying the deficits.

If employers must have cheap assistance, they should learn that the counting room is not the department to save in. Let them give their bookkeepers a better prospect than a pauper's grave, and they will have less reason to apprehend fraud.

A PHOTOCOPIED REPRODUCTION

OF

H. J. METTENHEIMER'S

SAFETY BOOK-KEEPING

OF

1875

PHOTOCOPIED FROM THE ORIGINAL BOOK
SUBMITTED FOR COPYRIGHT PROTECTION BY THE
AUTHOR TO THE LIBRARY OF CONGRESS

Important Books for Business Men!

Swan's New Treatise.
TENTH EDITION—1875.

A LA.. SUBSTAN-
.... .00.

All .... Men will
find t.. ir rights
and l...

Thi... ghts and
liabili... d selling
of bi'.. cks, and
banke.. s, principal a.. lating to
paym... audulent
conve.. ppage *in*
trans... ns, interest a... mortgage
of go... e claims,
mort... usemen's
recei.. s, Mortga-
ges, ... nt, Judgment

A Su... IE USE OF

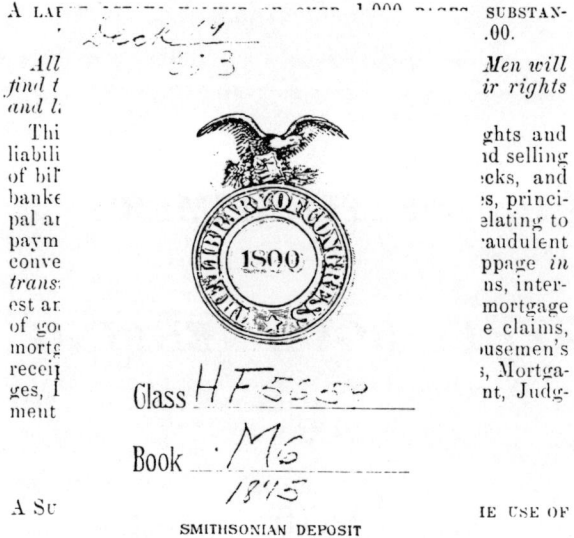

A .... , liabilities
and duties of partners, as concerns themselves and others,
with forms.

The above books will be sent by mail, free, on receipt of the price.

ROBERT CLARKE & CO., Publishers,
65 West Fourth Street, Cincinnati.

SAFETY BOOK-KEEPING

BEING

A COMPLETE EXPOSITION OF

BOOK-KEEPERS' FRAUDS

HOW COMMITTED!

HOW DISCOVERED!

HOW PREVENTED!

ALSO, CONTAINING

A SAFE METHOD OF MANAGING THE CASH DEPARTMENT OF RETAIL STORES

A CONVENIENT METHOD OF KEEPING

A PURCHASE ACCOUNT FOR COMMISSION HOUSES, AND A COLLECTION ACCOUNT FOR BAD DEBTS

WITH

OTHER SUGGESTIONS OF VALUE TO MERCHANTS AND BOOK-KEEPERS IN THE MANAGEMENT OF ACCOUNTS

BY

H. J. METTENHEIMER

CINCINNATI
ROBERT CLARKE & CO
1875

Entered according to Act of Congress, in the year 1869, by H. J. METTENHEIMER, in the Clerk's office of the District Court of the Eastern District of Pennsylvania.

COPYRIGHT 1875, BY H. J. METTENHEIMER.

CONTENTS.

Preface..	v
Introduction..	vii
Book-keepers' frauds....................................	12
Transposition of figures................................	16
Original ledger entries and false ledger balances.....	19
Petty cash-books..	21
Bill or note accounts...................................	24
City invoice-books......................................	27
Short cash...	29
Book-keeper's personal account........................	31
Pay-rolls...	33
Gold bills..	36
Collection account......................................	38
A well-known fraud.....................................	40
Salary signature book..................................	43
To prevent fraud in the cash department of retail stores..	45
To prevent fraud..	47
An apology for book-keepers...........................	53
Remedies at law for frauds in book-keeping...........	55
A check on hazardous credits..........................	60

(iii)

PREFACE TO THE PRESENT EDITION.

The first edition of this book was published in Philadelphia in 1869, and was intended as a card to introduce the author as an Auditor of Accounts. It was circulated privately and without charge. In offering the present edition to the public, the writer has been requested to consider the following objection to its indiscriminate distribution.

"If the work falls into the hands of book-keepers, it might teach them something of which they are ignorant, and impel them to do just what it is intended to prevent."

The fact is, however, that a man who is dishonest can always conceive methods of his own for committing crime without instruction, and a necessity therefore arises for EMPLOYERS to be informed of such conceptions, and provided with the means of preventing their execution.

People who are possessed of valuables are desirous of placing them where they will be secure. A business man's money is under lock and key to all except his book-keeper, and this work is presented as a lock and key against the book-keeper. Because the use of a preventive may be prostituted, it constitutes no reason to abolish the preventive, and an effectual guard against fraudulent book-keeping is greatly needed. Any project that will render an attempt to swindle unusually hazardous is a check to the evil. The author therefore contends that his book will deter more than it will ever incite to wrong-doing.

The design of this book is to point out where trouble in accounts arise; to show how they may be obviated; and to prevent its readers becoming victims to fraud.

THE AUTHOR

Has been a practical book-keeper for twenty years, has been in the employ of the following firms:

1855–57.	S. J. Bestor, Philadelphia, Pa.
1857.	J. H. Ashbridge & Nephew, New Orleans, La.
1858.	O'Dwyer & Doolittle, Montgomery, Ala.
1859–62.	W. H. Hannon & Bro., Montgomery, Ala.
1863.	Bank of Montgomery, Montgomery, Ala.
1864.	Central Iron Works, Shelby Co., Ala.
1865.	Duncannon Iron Works, Philadelphia, Pa.
1866–69.	Hannon, Offut & Co., New Orleans, La.
1870.	Dane, Westlake & Covert, Chicago, Ill.
1870.	R. Proctor, Philadelphia, Pa.
1871–75.	Babbitt, Harkness & Co., Cincinnati, O.
1875.	Victor Sewing Machine Co., Cincinnati, O.

He has also adjusted complicated accounts for other business houses from New York to Texas.

(vi)

INTRODUCTION.

As you can probably save more money by spending an hour in reading this little book than you ever made in the same time, your careful attention is directed to the following statement:

There are many merchants who only lack one qualification to conduct a business successfully, and they frequently suffer loss and bankruptcy without knowing the cause. The exception to their otherwise unexceptionable capacity is an ignorance of a method to govern their accounts.

More cases of insolvency are to be attributed to *fraudulent Book-keeping* than shrewd businessmen are aware of, and though the advice is almost universally unpopular, it is urged on merchants to overcome their disinclination for this species of labor, and give a little 'time to a thorough investigation of their books.

The author has been a book-keeper for twenty years, and has been employed in auditing complicated accounts in the principal cities of the Union. He is induced to submit the result of his wide experience to the consideration of all who are compelled to entrust their books to hired or partnership assistance.

That this trust is almost continually betrayed, is

too well known to need comment. Newspapers daily chronicle the detection of new cases of embezzlement, and still our merchants shut their eyes and believe it possible for all servants to be dishonest but their own. While they admit the shrewdness of their accountants in other matters, they blindly imagine them too trustworthy, or too fearful of consequences to deceive them in regard to a manipulation of their finances; yet in case of the death of an old favorite book-keeper, or even of a partner who has had the management of the cash, how often do we find that their apparently beautifully balanced accounts are teeming with a succession of fraudulent entries that have been continued through years.

It is a broad assertion to make—but a true one—that out of the large number of books I have examined, fully one-half contained palpable evidences of fraud, and in a majority of cases where there was no previous suspicion of anything wrong.

The most stupendous defalcations are perpetrated by *partners* who have acted as cashiers. What is called embezzlement in an employe, is known as a breach of trust when committed by a partner, and as such, is exempt from criminal prosecution. Did business-men know how many of their fraternity keep or have kept these lively skeletons in their counting-rooms, very few partners would be entrusted with a cash account with-

INTRODUCTION. 9

out being required to make a full and frequent exhibit of the condition of their trust.

Published defalcations are but a small fraction of the number really committed. Confidential relations existing between book-keepers and one or more of their employers, are the causes why so few embezzlement cases come to light. Most houses have secrets that they do not wish exposed, and in addition to having their own credit impaired by prosecuting a defaulter, they would have their weak places divulged in retaliation; hence, a great preponderance of frauds are always privately compromised.

You will acknowledge the truth of these statements, and say you are powerless to apply a remedy; that your manifold duties prevent you from attending to your counting-room; that you are ignorant of the technicalities of book-keeping, and can not discover errors even if so disposed. The object of this little pamphlet is to enable all concerned, whether they are conversant with the matter or not, *to audit their own accounts.*

The style is plain, the matter condensed, and the subject exhausted in these few pages. So much information was never before contained in so brief a space, and so useful and sure a guide was never more needed. After reading it, you may think the suggestions very appropriate, but imagine you can not spare the time to heed them. This is the rock on which many a proud commercial craft has gone to pieces, and on which you may swamp at any moment. It is therefore urged on you to try to give the matter your personal attention, and what has heretofore seemed a tangled labyrinth, will after a little practice become as clear and practicable as the noon-day sun. Nothing is easier to comprehend and master than a distasteful medley of figures after a few days trial. By spending a few moments each day over your books, you will be surprised how quickly you can accomplish what had hitherto occupied so long a time, and if you will reflect that your safety, your fortune, and your ultimate happiness almost entirely depend on your own care and scrutiny, you will no longer hesitate to overcome a personal dislike to the details of accounts.

Perhaps the safest prey for skillful book-keepers are parties who believe they are too proficient in the science to be swindled. The fault here is, that while a rogue will avoid a breaker known to all, and conform to such established forms as some employers prescribe as an absolute check to fraud, he will be operating in a channel of which his employer is ignorant. An accountant's brain is a fertile field for invention, and most of the old methods for fraud are so widely known that the imagined arbitrary remedies have become obsolete, except in the minds of employers, who consider themselves beyond learning anything new. To such, this little work is especially recommended, though it is doubtful whether they will not continue in the belief of their own infallibility.

One business at a time is enough for most mortals, and if you care for your legitimate occupation, it will not pay to trust it to subordinates and employ your own time in idleness, amusement or outside speculations. A cashier knows well enough when his principals are too much engaged in other pursuits to watch his actions very closely, and his assumed devotion to the interests of his employers is frequently only a cloak to cover his own rascality. If you can make one thousand dollars by kite-flying, while a clerk is stealing five thousand that might have been saved by your own vigilance, you are a heavy loser in the end, and will probably only learn better when too late. Admitting the worldly inhumanity of the advice to *trust no man*, it is well known that the most successful merchants are those who adopt so harsh and uncharitable a rule.

BOOK-KEEPERS' FRAUDS.

A FAVORITE idea with those who have nothing but a theoretical knowledge of Book-keeping is, that a Trial Balance proves the correctness of a Ledger, and the accuracy of every detail and posting before reaching the Ledger. In a treatise on the methods of embezzlement, it is necessary to explode this idea at the start. As will be explained hereafter, a Trial Balance taken from a defaulter's work proves nothing, unless it be a little expertness on the part of the operater in concealing intentional error.

The only benefit to be derived from frauds in accounts arises from a desire to absorb the *Cash*, so it follows that the greater part of the trouble in detecting errors may be obviated by examining the Cash Account only. Fully three-fourths of the remaining labor may be avoided by testing the additions, as a defrauder is in most cases particularly careful to make his original entries correctly. Strange as it may appear to a novice in auditing, it seldom pays to examine if the proper credits are given for cash payments, because errors of this kind are so liable to accidental detection that a first-class rogue would not attempt to make them.

BOOK-KEEPERS' FRAUDS.   13

In the additions or manipulation of the figures alone need employers hope to readily discover how they are swindled, and the first thing to do is to add the long columns of the Cash-book. Do this thoroughly, and if you fail to find the addition of the debit side $10, $100, or $1,000 too little, or the credit side $10, $100, or $1,000 too great, you can resort to our next plan.

You may argue that a book-keeper would not dare to do this because the discrepancy would appear in the Trial Balance. He can cover his tracks very easily, however, by making a corresponding error in the footings of the Journal, and if you examine your Merchandise, Expense, or any but a personal account, you will find a mistake on the contra side for the deficit in cash. Of course, two errors of the same amount, but on different sides, will result in a balance of the books. These forced balances and double mistakes are always intentional and never occur by accident.

As but few persons are expert in adding, the following plan may be of service to parties who are not skillful at the work: Run your columns both up and down, so one may prove the other. In casting up a page, place the total of first column down in pencil; carry all but the right-hand figure to the next column, and place the result of this column under the other, carrying all but the right hand figure to the next column, and so on until the page is complete. The entire figures of the last footing

SAFETY-BOOK-KEEPING.

and the units of the others will be the total of the page, thus:

```
        18294.12
        19183.01
        27096.20
        39172.21
        18096.12
        27171.03
        19096.11
        28184.00
        19075.20
        38196.13
        29082.01
        18198.14
        29073.20
        16299.10
        57182.31
        29396.12
        49183.24
        38692.33      5-3  first column.
        28394.06      3-4  second    "
        49088.27      11-4 third     "
        38394.26      21-1 fourth    "
        59287.15      5-1  fifth     "
        29184.01      20-3 sixth     "
        18096.10      74   seventh   "
Total...743114.43    743114.43
```

In a hasty addition of the foregoing, you are liable to the following errors:

In the *third* column, by carrying *one* instead of *eleven;* in the *fourth* column, by carrying *eleven* instead of *twenty-one;* in the *fifth* column, by carrying *fifteen* instead of *five;* and in the *sixth* column, by carrying *ten* instead of *twenty*.

TRANSPOSITION OF FIGURES.　　　15

Try this, and see how easy it is to get the total down wrong. Every one but experienced accountants frequently fail to carry enough figures after they reach one hundred, and it is right here where the book-keeper knows and possesses his advantage to make ten, one hundred, or one thousand dollars occasionally.

We would suggest that you require all cash footings penciled and left standing as in the example, and if your cashier is honest, he will not object to comply with the requirement.

TRANSPOSITION OF FIGURES.

Another easy plan to defraud, and one that is still more frequent than the preceding, is in the transposition of figures. The opportunities for so transposing them are legion, and as every occurrence of the kind may be covered in the Trial Balance by a corresponding transposition in some representative account, of course the much vaunted Trial Balance-sheet does not prove the correctness of the books.

It sometimes happens that figures are transposed by accident, but when this is the case, the accounts will fail to accord until the error is discovered and corrected. An accountant perceiving that an accidental fault of this kind has remained undetected for a long time by his employers, and then only found out by himself, becomes more venturesome thereafter, repeating the thing willfully and with intent to defraud. In the first instance there is no necessity for a contra error, and none will be discovered, but *willful mistakes are always twins.*

Suppose your cashier receives a payment of...$2979.00
And credits it on the Cash-book as.......... 2799.00

There is a difference of...................... $180.00

TRANSPOSITION OF FIGURES. 17

And he will have that much surplus when he counts what ought to be on hand.

Or suppose he enters an expenditure $3533.00
When he really paid but...................... 3353.00

Leaving as before............................ $180.00

which should appear as so much *over* when he balances the cash at night.

What employer would be apt to notice it, and what is to prevent the cashier from putting the surplus in his pocket? In such instances the original entry can be made wrong, while the *right figures may be posted*, and the discrepancy balanced or counteracted in "Merchandise" or some similar account. Experienced detectives have checked through a set of books, passing over instances of this apparently impossible chance for fraud, just because the figures looked and sounded as if they were correct.

Again, if, in *footing* a page of the
 Cash-book, the debtor side foots......$19789.00
And is carried forward.................... 17989.00
                                           ─────────
                                           $1800.00

Or the credit side is carried forward....$19789.00
When it only foots.......................... 17989.00
                                           ─────────
                                           $1800.00

it is palpable that the cashier has made a clean sweep of eighteen hundred dollars outside of his salary.

18   SAFETY BOOK-KEEPING.

To discover such errors, it is necessary for you to look over your Cash-book yourself, and to look with your eyes wide open. It is surprising how often you may look right at a mistake of this kind and yet fail to detect it.

The magnitude of the transposition of course depends on the extent of the business. It can be made on small as well as large amounts, and as often as your book-keeper considers it consistent with his own ideas of propriety. One instance came under my own observation in Philadelphia, where it appeared as if the *partner* who was *running the cash*, really thought he would do himself an injustice by making a correct entry.

ORIGINAL AND FALSE LEDGER ENTRIES.   19

ORIGINAL LEDGER ENTRIES AND FALSE LEDGER BALANCES.

In cases where a cashier fails to credit on the Cash-book money received from a customer, a very ugly manner of concealing the delinquency is, to place the credit directly on the Ledger, without permitting it to get there through the proper channels. Or a cashier may receive money, and neither enter nor post it anywhere at all, merely drawing his red ink lines in the Ledger under the account involved, and footing the different sides alike when they do not add up alike.

These contrivances necessitate counteracting errors in other places, and "Merchandise" is generally the object selected to suffer.

To discover the aggregate of such embezzlements, it is necessary to test the virtue of every balance on your Ledger, and to examine every entry, footing, posting, and balance that has any connection with your "Merchandise account" on every book in use. "Merchandise" may have been doctored in the Journal (or on the Sales-book and Invoice-book, in case you do not journalize your sales and purchases); or in transit from any of these books to the Ledger; or the errors may

20   SAFETY BOOK-KEEPING.

have been covered in footing or balancing the account in the Ledger. You will be required to compare the entries with the postings, and make a Check-mark (✓) to every original entry; a similar mark to every posting, and one to every footing and balance, as you find them correct. The sum of such as are not checked will be the total amount of frauds of this class that have been covered as suggested.

As this method of swindling is more liable to accidental detection than any other, it is not of very frequent occurrence. I would not therefore recommend a search requiring so much labor, unless you are convinced that you are harboring a scamp in your counting-room, and are anxious to fasten some act upon him. It is a bungling method of concealing financial absorption, and is mainly resorted to by partners who can plead press of other duties as an excuse for their *carelessness*.

PETTY CASH-BOOKS.

THESE books have become quite an institution in houses doing any Cash business, and like all other auxiliary and labor-saving devices, are not to be depended on for correctness.

On one side are entered all sales made for cash, and the total amount of these sales is entered in the large Cash-book to the credit of Merchandise, at the end of the month, and from there posted into the Ledger. On the contra side are entered all small items of expense, such as freight, drayage, stationery, gas, water, advertising, and other bills of similar import. At the end of the month this side is dissected, and the total amounts entered on the large Cash-book, to be posted on the accounts to which they apply. The opportunities these books afford for dishonesty are as follows:

You are really keeping two Cash-books, and it is common for peculating cashiers to charge items of expense twice on the same book, or once in the Petty Cash-book and once in the large Cash-book. A freight-bill can be charged once by itself, and then charged again by merging it with some others, For instance:

By freight on 10 hogsheads sugar............... 36.00
By freight paid C. H. & D. R. R................ 75.00

That is, the charge for $75 may contain the freight for the ten hogsheads of sugar previously entered. Or you might consult your main Cash-book and find

By freight paid C. H. & D. R. R................ 75.00

entered on it as well as on the Petty Cash-book.

Only one side of this Book, however, is kept by *Double* Entry in this manner; the other side frequently dispensing with any entry at all.

When a bill is paid before the entry is posted from the Sales-book, it is customary to mark the same *paid*, and the amount is omitted in the monthly footing of that Book. This is very correct, provided the payment is entered as a Cash Sale on the Petty Cash-book, and you should see that this is never forgotten. The date of payment should be placed on the Sales-book at the same time the entry is marked paid, and you had better compare these marks with the Petty Cash-book regularly at the end of every month, and see that your Cash has been debited with the money in every instance.

Incorrect additions are fearfully frequent in these books, and as the errors are not revealed in a Trial Balance, no counteracting entries are necessary. There is no check on them except the eye of the employer, and if he consents to permit their use, it is his own fault if he is cheated. The fact

PETTY CASH-BOOKS.

is, these books are considered of so little moment that they are rarely inspected by anybody, and when filled up, are frequently lost sight of entirely. It is to the interest of a dishonest book-keeper that they be destroyed when they have fulfilled their mission, and very few houses could collect an unbroken succession of them.

Even in case they are kept, a book-keeper who apprehends they will be looked over at some future time, can alter the figures to agree with the wrong additions on them. This is pretty safe work after a sufficient time has elapsed for an employer to forget the probable circumstances of the transactions, and of course this tampering would then escape his scrutiny.

BILL OR NOTE ACCOUNTS.

Some concerns doing a very heavy note business never think of going any further than striking a balance on these accounts when they wish to ascertain the amount in notes due them, or how much they owe in outstanding paper of their own. If their books are kept correctly, this balance of course will give them the information desired, but it is just as often that false entries have been made here as elsewhere. If you are in the habit of giving a note for every bill purchased from houses with whom you deal often, your cashier may have a habit of charging cash with a note every now and then that you have never given, and which never existed. Even if you daily examine your Cash-book, you will not be apt to look too closely at an entry, "By Bills Payable, paid John Jones' note due this day," when similar entries are of almost daily occurrence. You will naturally take it for granted that this note is one of the many you have given John Jones, when perhaps if you refer to your Note-book you will discover that there was none due on this day, and that the amount so charged is a fraud.

To test the correctness of your Bills Payable ac-

BILL OR NOTE ACCOUNTS. 25

count, you should add the amount of notes remaining unpaid on the Note-book, and this must agree with the credit balance of your Bills Payable account on the Ledger. When *paid*, all notes should be retained, and numbered and filed away as vouchers in the same manner as ordinary receipts, so they can be forthcoming whenever demanded for auditing.

If you are in the habit of hiring money from Banks, you should also occasionally get from their Note-clerks a list of such notes as they hold against you and compare it with your own record. This may appear a work of supererogation, but the writer knows of an instance in which a Bank was discounting a firm-note with sixty day renewals for $5000, made by a financiering partner, the proceeds of which had never appeared in his Cash-book. This note was originally made to cover an absorption of cash for personal uses that had been continued a long time before it was discovered.

To test the correctness of your Bills Receivable account, the amount of all notes or acceptances you hold in your possession should agree with the debit balance of the Bills Receivable account on the Ledger.

The safest, best, and most convenient way of keeping Note Accounts is the *Linear System*. By this method each note is posted on a separate line in the Ledger page, and whenever one is paid, the payment is posted on the contra side of the same line. Then, when you wish to know the number and amount of those unpaid, you have only to count the unbalanced spaces. For instance:

Bills Receivable.

Jan. 1. To White & Black..$1 500	Aug. 1. By cash,.................$1500
" 6. To John Jones......... 200	
Mar. 5. To Martin & Moore 800	Sept. 15. By cash............... 800
Apr. 10. To Wm. Skeezix.... 700	
Aug. 7. To Geo. Ellis......... 500	
Sept. 11. To Jno. Sullivan... 900	Dec. 14. By cash............... 900

Here the balance due you on notes is $1400
The spaces unbalanced are:
          John Jones................................. $200
          Wm. Skeezix............................. 700
          George Ellis............................... 500
                                                  $1400

Or,

Bills Payable.

Sept. 6. To cash.................$1200	Jan. 1. By Hayes & Young.$1200
	Feb. 6. By Peter Williams.. 500
	Apr. 7. By Third Nat. Bank 5000
Oct. 3. To cash............... 1400	July 10. By Allen & Cary...... 1400
	Sept. 5. By First Nat. Bank. 2500
Dec. 13. To cash............... 3000	Oct. 10. By A. T. Stuart....... 3000

Here the amount you owe on outstanding paper is.................$8000
The spaces unbalanced are:
          Peter Williams............................$ 500
          Third National Bank.................. 5000
          First National Bank................... 2500
                                                 $8000

By this method, which is employed by all honest and skillful accountants who have ever tried it, no difficulty is occasioned in discovering at a glance how much is due you, and by whom; and how much you owe, and to whom, on unmatured or dishonored paper.

CITY INVOICE-BOOKS.   27

CITY INVOICE-BOOKS.

The City Invoice-book is another device to shirk the labor of posting, and though it possesses no objectionable feature if kept honestly, it still offers such brilliant opportunities for theft, as to warrant either its discontinuance or a decided limitation of its use.

There are so many houses established which carry only special lines of goods that very few general concerns will attempt to compete with them in a jobbing way. They prefer buying just enough from the specialists to fill their daily orders, and so an immense number of small bills are accumulated during a month. To avoid filling a Ledger too rapidly with these trifling postings, the City Invoice-book was adopted, the purpose being to aggregate at the end of the month all bills purchased from each particular house, and post it *en masse* to the credit of that house. If this purpose was adhered to, there could be no objection to the book, but its sphere is gradually being extended far beyond the original intention for which it was designed.

At present many book-keepers never journalize from the City Invoice-book at all, but settle the bills before they enter the Ledger. The amount due each house is footed up, paid, and then "Merchandise" is debited on the Cash-book with the payment. By this manner "Merchandise" can be debited with just as much more than was ever bought, as will meet the requirements of a dishonest cashier's pocket. After a monthly settlement with a house, a book-keeper can commence on the account on the City Invoice-book, raise the amount of some bills, interline others, and swell the total to suit himself. He may have paid out $250, and charged cash with $550, thus saving $300 for himself. You may argue that the receipt taken for the payment would prevent this, but if you will look at your receipt-book, you will find the majority of such receipts written in a very slovenly manner, and therefore *susceptible of alteration*.

The remedy is to have the totals of every account that is opened on the City Invoice-book posted on your Ledger at the end of the month to the credit of the houses from whom the purchases were made. Then, when you suspect anything wrong, it is much easier to compare accounts with the parties from whom you buy, than attempt to reconcile the discrepancies on a record that can be altered whenever convenient.

SHORT CASH.

An instance has recently come under the notice of the writer, wherein a cashier, at a final settlement with a firm, was short over $10,000 in the balance of money that should have been on hand. The presumption is that this shortage had been growing for years, and its concealment for so long a time was only made possible by the extreme confidence that had been reposed in the defaulter by his principals. No fraudulent entries had been made to cover the deficiency, and it was only discovered upon a dissolution of partnership. In the whole time of this defaulter's stewardship, no call had ever been made on him for an exhibit of what his purported balances consisted. As the sum of the default was daily growing larger, however, it became necessary to prevent so great a balance appearing, and this was accomplished by merely withholding for a few days some large credits from the Cash-book. In case the cashier in question had a note discounted in bank, the proceeds of said note would appear on his Note-book and on the margin of his Checkbook, but would probably not be placed on the Cash-book for several days, or even weeks after the money thus realized had been checked upon.

30   SAFETY BOOK-KEEPING.

Or in case of receiving heavy remittances during a day, he would withhold entering the larger checks, although he would deposit them to make the balance he should have had. On the next arrival of large receipts, he would enter up the old credits that were omitted, and neglect to enter the new ones. By these really bungling contrivances he managed to keep such a balance continually exhibited as would create no suspicion.

The parties who suffered by this default made the mistake of allowing their cashier too much rope. They never asked him for a statement of what money he had on hand, and in fact never had, nor desired access to his Bank or Check books.

A remedy for this Short Cash delinquency would be to require, every night, a complete analyzed statement prepared of what your cashier's balance consists—how much in bank, in the drawer, on the Petty Cash-book, on personal memoranda, etc.

These statements should be entered in detail on printed and dated blanks, securely bound, and should be religiously kept for future reference. They will serve as a check upon delayed entries and false exhibits; as a comparison between them and your Cash, Bank, or Check books would reveal doctoring, if any had been employed, on very short investigation.

BOOK-KEEPER'S PERSONAL ACCOUNT.

In investigating suspicious accounts, it is frequently discovered that book-keepers have taken money from the Cash Drawer, charged it to themselves (probably before their employer's eyes), and then deliberately posted the item to "Merchandise" or "Expense." Hence, it might pay to see if your cashier's monetary supplies always appear to his debit on the Ledger.

Also examine his account for the purpose of ascertaining the sources from which he places money *to his credit.* While no objection might be urged to a book-keeper speculating in produce, shaving notes, or buying real estate on his own account, there is no particular necessity for his keeping the run of such transactions on *your* Ledger. Such accounts sometimes get badly mixed, and you would do well to restrict his personal account on your books to matters appertaining to his relations with you.

It would do no harm to occasionally inquire into your book-keeper's style of living, and see if it corresponds with the salary he is getting. If an unmarried man, you can judge by his associates whether he is spending more than he earns. If

32   SAFETY BOOK-KEEPING.

married, a visit to his place of residence might throw considerable light on how much it would require to maintain his establishment. While anything like a sneaking surveillance is to be condemned, a little sociability with an employe, in order to learn his habits, is certainly to be commended in an employer.

PAY-ROLLS.

Manufacturers and dealers who employ a large number of journeymen and clerks, do not pretend to keep personal accounts with them all in their Ledger. The practice has been to enter and pay the wages due each person on the Pay-roll, and charge the total to Merchandise, Expense, or Labor.

Now, some of these concerns are in the habit of giving their employes orders for dry-goods, groceries, and other supplies, upon parties with whom they are trading, and deducting the amount of such orders from the wages of the party to whom they are given.

By this arrangement a book-keeper is afforded a chance to convert to his own use, either the entire amount of the orders issued, or as much of it as he may deem prudent. He can simply charge the whole, or as much of the Pay-roll as he pleases, on his Cash-book, when enough of it to represent the full sum of the orders should be charged on other books.

To avoid this, an account headed "Pay-roll" should be opened on the Ledger. Charge the account with every order that is issued, and credit it to the dealer on whom it is drawn. Credit " Pay-

34   SAFETY-BOOK-KEEPING.

roll Account" with the total footing of each Pay-roll, debiting the same to Labor, Expense, or Merchandise. Now, when the hands are paid off, charge the account, on the Cash book with the actual money required to settle the difference between the orders issued and the total amount of the Pay-roll. This should produce a balance on the account in the Ledger, if kept correctly. To illustrate the Journal entries:

Labor Account, Dr.
              To Pay-roll Account.
For wages due for week ending September 10th...$320.00

Pay-roll Account, Dr.
              To Sundries..
To A. T. Stewart & Co. (For order issued upon them in favor of Wm. Allen) $22.00
To Wm. Glenn & Sons. (For order issued upon them in favor of Thos. Jones)......... 14.00
To Burckhardt & Co. (For order issued upon them in favor of Wm. Tompkins)... 12.00
To Peebles & Co. (For order issued upon them in favor of J. Williams)...... .... 18.00
                                                                $66.00

This leaves $254 to be paid for wages *in money*, and the entry on the Cash-book should be for this amount and no more. When these entries are all posted, it will produce a balance on the "Pay-roll Account," which is thus closed for the week.

PAY-ROLLS. 35

Whether you are in the habit of giving orders or not, you should in all cases require this "Pay-roll Account" opened on your Ledger. It will be easier to compare it in the future with your Pay-rolls, than be compelled to look all through your books for entries appertaining to them.

Concerning the integrity of the Pay-roll itself, but little can be said. Firms or corporations employing a large number of hands are always more or less at the mercy of their assistants. Collusion between them and the operatives can not be prevented by book-keeping. Principals must devise their own system of espionage to keep sinecures and inflated wages off their Rolls. It would do no harm to require the signatures of both the journeyman, clerk, or laborer getting the money, and of the department manager or section "boss," on the line representing each particular payment, but this would not be an infallible remedy where a determination to steal existed.

You can depend upon nothing but your own vigilance for protection from Pay-roll frauds.

GOLD BILLS.

Importers and dealers in foreign merchandise are in the habit of charging goods to their customers at so much *in gold*. This is rendered necessary on account of the fluctuation that may take place in the price of gold between the date of sale and the date of payment. The first debit is at a gold price, and when the bill is paid, a second debit should be made, charging the buyer with the premium required to convert the gold into currency. In many cases, however, the customer is only credited with the amount of his bill in gold, and the balance of his remittance, representing the premium, is *supposed* to be credited to "Merchandise." A book-keeper is here afforded an opportunity to absorb the amount of the premium by omitting the latter ceremony altogether, and as there is no charge to any personal account for the premium, the matter is not likely to be discovered.

The remedy is simple:

Require the amount of the premium in every instance to be charged to the customer on the date the gold is covered. This will make it a necessity to give him credit for the whole of his remittance in order to balance the account. I would suggest

GOLD BILLS. 37

that you have alternate lines left blank on the account in your Ledger, where you are in the habit of selling the same party two or more bills before any one of them is settled. These lines can be used to post the premium items under the bills to which they relate, and leave the accounts in more artistic shape than they would be by continuous posting.

These frauds are susceptible of a back-action movement, as the buyer is liable to be swindled on his side of the transaction.

His gold invoices are credited to the party from whom they were bought at a gold price. When the rate of gold is determined, a second credit is made on the Journal to the seller's account, for the amount of the premium. Now, when the bill is paid, the seller is charged with the full amount of the check remitted, and the charging should stop here. I have, however, seen cases where "Merchandise" was charged *on the Cash-book* with the premium, after the charge to the seller's account had already closed the transaction. This made two charges for the price paid for the gold, the amount of one going into the book-keeper's pocket.

The only way to avoid this is to watch every entry bearing on gold payments, and never permit premium entries on the Cash-book at all.

38   SAFETY BOOK-KEEPING.

COLLECTION ACCOUNT.

AFTER a business has been continued for some years, a difficulty is encountered in keeping track of bad debts. Such as are known to be worthless are very properly thrown into "Profit and Loss" at the end of a year, and pass out of notice. Such as there exists a hope of realizing something upon in the future, are gathered together under a "Suspense Account." There still remains a class of notes and accounts upon which suit has been brought with a sure prospect of collection. These are generally scattered all over the Ledger, and very frequently remain in their original position without any remarks concerning what has been done with them. I have known numbers of such accounts charged to "Profit and Loss" by a change of book-keepers, and then fade from the memory of everybody connected with the house. In many instances some of these accounts have already been collected by attorneys, who have failed to make the proper returns of the money, and who are perhaps trusting to their luck in their clients having forgotten them. Whether this is often the case or not, it is easier to watch such accounts under *one head* than under a different head for

COLLECTION ACCOUNT.   39

each different note or account. I would therefore suggest that you purge the different pages of your Ledger of such claims as are already in litigation, and bring them together under a new head, called "Collection Account." Then, whenever you send other claims to an attorney, have an entry made at once, charging the same to this "Collection Account." You thus have all your bad debts that are in suit continually under your eyes, where they can be watched through the slow process of suit, judgment, stay, and execution, without being obliged to look all through your Ledger for them.

The entries should be sufficiently explanatory on the Ledger. Thus:

Collection Account.

Jan. 1. To John Jones.............$750
      In hands of Smith &
      Brown, Attorneys,
      Newark, O.
Aug. 1. To Wm. Young........$300
      In hands of Gull &
      Co., Attorneys, Lexington, Ky.	

This plan will recommend itself to any one who has hunted all over a Ledger to find the accounts, and then all through a Letter-book to find the name of the attorney, whenever he wished to write and ascertain the condition of such claims.

A WELL-KNOWN FRAUD.

It has previously been shown how "Merchandise Account" was made a cover for a heavy proportion of all the willful errors in book-keeping. Those made by experts through this channel have already been commented upon. To render this little work more complete, it is necessary to speak of a very common swindle that is practiced by *amateur* rascals. Every employer, except such as know nothing of the principles of double-entry book-keeping, is aware of this process, and its frequent perpetration can only be attributed to the ignorance or gross carelessness of those who are victimized by it. This article will therefore be made as clear and simple as possible, so as to be comprehended by any man of ordinary business capacity.

When *money* is received, it should be entered on the left-hand side of your Cash-book. When *goods* are received, they should be entered on your Invoice-book, and afterward journalized. One or more bills that you purchase are generally recorded together, under a head-line of "Merchandise, Dr. To Sundries."

Now, a dishonest book-keeper who receives

money, can omit to enter it on the left-hand side of the Cash-book, and yet produce the same result in the Ledger as if he had placed it where it properly belonged. He merely enters the credit in his Journal under this head-line of " Merchandise, Dr. To Sundries." Whenever this is done, you lose just that much *Cash*, and yet the customer's account on the Ledger will have credit for the amount. At the end of the month, your bookkeeper will present you with a perfect Trial Balance Sheet, and you will conclude that everything is correct.

You need not study book-keeping to prevent this. As a general thing you do not buy from and sell to the same parties. You know pretty well from whom you do buy, and you can examine all the names appearing under the head of " Merchandise, Dr. To Sundries." If you find there the name of any party you sell to, you should ascertain whether he has *returned* any goods purchased from you. If he has not, inquire into the reason for the entry. If your book-keeper's reply is evasive, you had better inquire directly of the customer whether he did not make a cash payment of a similar amount, that should, but does not appear on your Cashbook. If he did, your book-keeper's receipt for the money will be the concluding link in the evidence against him of intent to embezzle the amount. Satisfy yourself of the integrity of these entries in every instance, if you have any suspicion that you

42   SAFETY BOOK-KEEPING.

are being defrauded; for when it is once commenced, this system of cheating will grow very rapidly if not checked.

In cases where you do buy from and sell to the same parties. you should, at the end of the month, make a practice of calling for every bill that you purchase, and then compare them with every entry under this head of "Merchandise, Dr. To Sundries." If any names appear for which you have no bills, explanations will be in order as before.

SALARY SIGNATURE-BOOK.   43

SALARY SIGNATURE-BOOK.

WHILE the growing tendency to employ labor-saving books is greatly to be deprecated, the adoption of a " Salary Signature-book " is recommended to every firm who keep their own or their clerks' personal accounts on the Ledger. Any small blank book with a single money column will answer the purpose. On this book the members of the firm and the employees sign their names whenever they receive money from your cashier, extending the amount to the money column themselves. These entries are not posted until the end of the month, when the different sums drawn by each man are collected together and entered on the Cash-book in one amount. Of course, in balancing the cash at night, the amount represented on this book will have to be considered as so much on hand.

One merit of this book is that it saves your Ledger. Some clerks will draw a little money every day, which would occupy thirty lines of your Ledger every month, when one line will answer the purpose.

Another merit is, that it saves work, as your book-keeper can do as much in this way by one posting as he otherwise could by thirty.

44   SAFETY BOOK-KEEPING.

The last recommendation is, that it saves disputes. If an employe think his account has grown too rapidly, and doubts the honesty or accuracy of the book-keeper, the difficulty can be adjusted by a reference to the " Salary Signature-book."

TO PREVENT FRAUD IN THE CASH DEPARTMENT OF RETAIL STORES.

MANY storekeepers have been utterly ruined by their cashiers, even while their establishments enjoyed a good run of custom, and the business was otherwise conducted on paying principles. Quite a number of plans for checking and counterchecking a day's cash sales have been devised, and without commenting on them all, I would recommend the following safe and simple method as the best:

The Cash Drawer should be handled by one person only. Not even the head of a firm should be allowed a key to it, as even where he is willing to assume any loss that might arise by his own carelessness, he places the regular custodian of the money in a state of nervous uncertainty whenever the balance is incomplete.

The salesmen should be furnished with books of *three*, instead of *two* printed blanks, each one of which should be numbered; the three on each page being numbered alike. When sales are made, the clerk fills out each of these three blanks, retaining the left-hand one or stub, and tearing the other two out of the book. One of these should be given to the cashier with the money, and the other dropped into a narrow slit cut in a locked box, the key of which should be kept by the proprietor. The box should be placed in a convenient location, so the cash-boys can insert the triplicates without causing any extra delay.

The merit of this plan is, that everything is completed on the spur of the moment; and the fact that one ticket has gone beyond the reach of being destroyed or tampered with, precludes the possibility of connivance between cashier and salesman to alter figures at their leisure during the day.

Of course, the amount of the day's sales ought to equal the sum of the tickets in the box, which should be counted nightly by the proprietor.

Under the old duplicate blank system an employer is so often cheated by reputed errors in sales, when evidences of alteration occur, that we think it best for him to attend to such changes himself, even if our method is adopted. In cases of error, or of money refunded for goods returned, we would advise that all such claims be submitted to one of the heads of the establishment, who alone should place in the ticket-box all slips referring to drawbacks.

TO PREVENT FRAUD.

It is so easy a thing to prevent fraudulent book-keeping, that it is really surprising to find so many merchants become the victims to this species of dishonesty. All men of good commercial capacity find it necessary to reduce the different departments of their business to a system, and, as a general thing, require a strict observance of their regulations from their employes. The one exception to this vigilance seems to be exactly where such vigilance is most required; and the apathy of business classes to the subject of their accounts is the more singular, from the fact that correct records are of the utmost importance to a knowledge of their own solvency. This apathy can not arise from indifference to office affairs. It is either ignorance of book-keeping, or a modest disinclination to interfere in the irksome details of the desk, that causes first-class business-men to lose money, while their cashiers are growing rich.

By requiring from the occupants of their counting-rooms, a strict adherence to the following suggestions, principals can thoroughly close up all the channels of fraud, and we are satisfied a little reflection will cause their universal adoption.

48   SAFETY BOOK-KEEPING.

Order is heaven's first law, and the science of accounts is founded on this law. Books of account are, or should be, a history of all transactions relating directly or indirectly to your finances. To record the events of this history in a careful manner, so you will remember the circumstance at any time in the future, is one object in keeping commercial books. All entries, therefore, should be clear, full, and explicit; much verbiage is unnecessary, but enough should be stated to render each record incapable of perversion or misconstruction. If you merely enter "Bills Payable, Dr., To Cash, $5.000," and post it without further explanation, you can not tell in a year after the entry is made whose note was paid, without referring to your Note-book; but if you only subjoin, "For John Smith's note, maturing this day," you can turn to the original entry made when the note was given, and learn what you are paying your $5.000 for. Without some such short statement following each entry, your book-keeper might give you any answer to inquiries about suspicious matters that best suited the description of fraud he was attempting to cover.

Have numerical lines ruled in the money columns of your books; for any accountant can render your attempt to investigate the integrity of his arithmetic almost an impossibility by slovenly numeration; placing units under tens, tens under hundreds, and hundreds under thousands. Apparent carelessness in this particular is frequently designed rascality.

Audit your own Cash-book during the dull season of every year. This seems like a very heavy undertaking, and one from which most merchants will recoil at the first impulse. It can be simplified, however, so as to make it rather an easy and pleasant summer recreation. For every payment that is made, a receipt or voucher should be taken. Make this an absolute duty with your cashier. This voucher should be numbered, and a corresponding number placed on the entry relating to it. The vouchers should be filed carefully away in their proper order, and when the time is at hand for auditing, every voucher should be forthcoming. The work of comparing can then be accomplished very rapidly, and a few days will suffice to check up the entire cash business of a year. You should have a voucher for every entry, and be very careful that the same one, or a duplicate of it, is not palmed off on you for two distinct entries. By a little practice in our rules for addition previously given, you can soon become sufficiently expert in adding a column to go through every page of your Cash-book in a day or two more. When you reflect how this course may save you as much as the rest of your year's profits, we think the junior partners of large business houses will not hesitate to utilize our plan.

Have your Bills Receivable, Bills Payable, Profit

50   SAFETY BOOK-KEEPING.

and Loss, Suspense, and Collection Accounts posted to your Ledger *in detail.* The popular system of posting several entries in one should never be permitted on these accounts, or they will surely be used by dishonest book-keepers to cover accounts or entries that do not belong to them.

Keep an exact duplicate of the Petty Cash-book yourself; that is, have a book exactly like it, and take a copy every night of the daily items and footings from the one in your book-keeper's possession. This certainly will not occupy more than five minutes daily, and it is an effectual check against backward tampering.

Have every item composing a Bank Deposit entered in detail on the margin of your Check-book. This will serve to settle any difference of opinion existing between your customers and your book-keeper in regard to alleged payments of which your books contain no record. If a check or draft corresponding to a payment claimed to have been made, appears on the margin on the date it is said to have been made, the presumption is against your cashier. If no such amount is found there, you will be warranted in insisting on a repayment.

At the end of every month, after your book-keeper has made his final entries and incorporated into the main Cash-book the amounts represented in the Petty Cash and Salary Signature-books, you should call for a full exhibit of what constitutes your "Balance on Hand." To verify this, it will

TO PREVENT FRAUD. 51

be necessary for you to have your bank-book balanced in bank, and the sum there left to your credit, together with what is in the Cash Drawer, should correspond with this "Balance on Hand." Do not trust to appearances, but count the money yourself, and see that you really have what you are supposed to have. If National Bank Tellers can deceive Government Examiners with an appearance of correctness, it is possible that your book-keeper can deceive you in the same manner. If your cashier is a partner, it will be well to examine your bank book to see if it required a "Discount" of which you have no record, to make the balance shown on it.

Be honest yourself, and do not stoop to small swindling for trifling gains. Never use stamps twice, and never keep money received by error in counting. Book-keepers remember these petty cheats, and treasure the recollection for the purpose of a counter-charge in case of a threatened prosecution for fraud.

Pay the man who takes care of your money a salary sufficient for his family's support. If you hear of any real estate purchases, diamond investments, gambling transactions, sexual indiscretions, or other speculations of your book-keeper, it would profit you to ascertain how and where he derives the means to operate with. If you suspect that your own Cash Drawer is the source, or that your money is maintaining an extravagant expenditure

52   SAFETY-BOOK-KEEPING.

not commensurate with the salary you are paying, you had better discharge the man, and hire one who can live within the amount you are willing to allow him. If your business profits are too small to meet the demands of a competent and trustworthy assistant, you will find it to your interest to do your own work. " The laborer is worthy of his hire," and if he does not get it one way, he will another.

AN APOLOGY FOR BOOK-KEEPERS.

IF there exists any excuse for fraud, book-keepers are entitled to it.

As a general thing, the profession is too poorly paid, considering the sacrifice of health, the necessity of maintaining a gentlemanly appearance, and the poor prospect of advancement. To do his whole duty, a book-keeper is obliged to confine himself to the distasteful monotony of his employment in a manner that will speedily convert him into a mechanical overworked drone. He sees his principal preach honesty and practice fraud; and perceiving that dishonesty prospers in spite of the frightful stories to the contrary, concludes that it is easier to steal money than to earn it. He soon learns that where one swindle is published, a hundred remain undiscovered, and so is led to appropriate whatever he can to his own use. He knows that if a stone is thrown at him, he can throw a heavier one back; and if his employers are too blind to place his salary at a deserving figure, he considers himself justifiable for secretly supplying the deficits.

If employers must have cheap assistance, they

54   SAFETY BOOK-KEEPING.

should learn that the counting room is not the department to save in. Let them give their book-keepers a better prospect than a pauper's grave, and they will have less reason to apprehend fraud.

REMEDIES AT LAW FOR FRAUDS IN BOOK-KEEPING.

The law affords parties who have been victimized by fraudulent book-keeping very little chance for redress, and this fact is known to but few merchants except those who have already had recourse to the courts for restitution or revenge in such cases. If a knowledge of the obloquy entailed on the perpetrator, and of the difficulty he will encounter in obtaining employment in the future, is not satisfaction enough to the victim, he should be well prepared with an abundance of testimony before commencing a criminal action. A prosecutor who enters court with his own assurance of having been swindled as his strongest card, is frequently surprised to learn that what is a very clear case of embezzlement to him, can not always be made equally apparent to the average jury. Again, there are not many lawyers, or even judges, possessed of a sufficiently comprehensive acquaintance with accounts to thoroughly master a tangled case of this class of fraud. If a defendant is determined to make a bold fight, and can command the services of clever counsel, it is an easy task for the two to work on the ignorance of both judge and jury, and by acting on their sympathy, obtain a verdict opposed to good sense and a technical acquaintance with the situation.

This subject is claiming the attention of several eminent jurists in Great Britain, and the following extract from an article in a recent number of the *London Law Magazine* may not be inappropriate:

"An effectual means of promoting the speedy administration of justice, would probably be found in the more frequent reference of ill-digested and complicated cases to a special office. Cases are sometimes sent to court in a complete muddle. They fail naturally. The usual reply is, 'A man is bound to prove his own case,' which is very true as far as it goes, but does not cover the whole question. A court no doubt, may order a man who is responsible to others, to render an account, but that is just what no court can enforce effectually. He swears he has done his best, and it is impossible to prove the negative. What is really required in the class of cases referred to, is thoroughly skilled investigation. Now, though no doubt many lawyers are to be found who are good men of business, the practice of law does not afford good training for special work of this kind. Surely there is often a failure of justice from the want of such a power of investigation as might be afforded by a trained body of accountants, though their duties would extend beyond the mere adjustment of figures."

REMEDIES AT LAW, ETC.   57

To show how easily justice may be thwarted in even a clear case of defaulting, it is only necessary to instance the result of a case in which a notorious Massachusetts politician was counsel for the defaulter.

The teller of a New Haven bank requested advice in regard to what course he should follow to protect him from justice for a heavy embezzlement of the funds of the bank. He was told to simply deliver his keys to the cashier without making an exhibit of his " Balance on Hand." The cashier fell into the trap, and the question was then raised. " To whose custody was the deficit attributable?" As this question could not be decided, the defaulter escaped.

Where a partner is the defendant, the remedy is still more uncertain. There is no penal punishment for the offense, because the law does not recognize a partnership fraud as a crime. It is known as a Breach of Trust, and is exempt therefore from criminal prosecution. Where the default is susceptible of proof, the victim can have recourse to a civil suit after the partnership has been dissolved, but it is rare that anything can ever be found to satisfy a judgment obtained in such cases. The product of fraud is usually expended in fast living; but if a partner really has retained anything acquired by dishonesty, he is generally shrewd enough to conceal its whereabouts. The writer knows of a recent instance where a defaulting partner confessed judgment for the amount of his default (something over $10,000), in order to avoid the publicity of a trial, but when an attempt was made to levy on some property he was supposed to possess, it was discovered that he had passed the title long before.

A recent decision taken from a late number of the American Law Register will be of interest to copartners, but whether it will govern in Breaches of Trust by a fellow-partner is rather questionable.

"One partner can not apply the partnership funds or securities to the discharge of his own private debt without the consent of the other partners, either expressed or implied. Nor does it make any difference whether such creditor knew that it was partnership property or not that was thus applied in payment of his debt." Caldwell *v.* Scott and Trustee, 54 N. H.

It certainly seems strange that one man can steal from another without incurring any risk of punishment, and it seems still more strange that this immunity should be enjoyed by the very class least deserving of it. A heavy majority of merchants all over the country would ask for a speedy revision of the statutes, were they aware of their defect in this respect. The reason assigned by lawyers for the deficiency is, that a law compelling partners to be honest among themselves, would have a tendency to destroy partnerships. Hence, parties who have had their confidence betrayed, and their money

REMEDIES AT LAW, ETC.   59

stolen by a partner, and who lack the muscular ability to redress the grievance, can console themselves with the old axiom that " Partnerships are the worst ships a man can sail in."

A CHECK ON HAZARDOUS CREDITS.

For six months or a year preceding, a "Commercial Crisis," it is generally found that less care was shown in scrutinizing credits than is customary at other periods. Although merchants knew that a financial panic was approaching, and that even good accounts should have been restricted, yet the desire to sell goods at this time was so great that they not only permitted an unlimited growth to old customers, but gave credit to parties totally unworthy of it. It seems strange that those who have hitherto used sound judgment in this respect should forget that "depreciating stock is better than worthless accounts," at the very time their judgment is most needed. A late circular issued by R. G. Dun & Co., contains the following remark:

"An undue expansion of credits for the purpose of inducing business is an evil policy at any time, but it is peculiarly so, when economy, restricted trade, and gradual reduction of existing indebtedness should be the features of the hour. Cheap credit is the sure precursor of disaster; and, while the strongest element in the financial fabric in these trying times has been the small indebtedness, it is

A CHECK ON HAZARDOUS CREDITS.

not difficult to see that, if the lines of credit become lax, in time, amount, or character, all that now promises favorably will only contribute to hasten an unhealthy and an unsafe condition of business. If, on the contrary, a wise conservatism is practiced in this respect—if the standard of credit is elevated rather than lowered, and a rigid scrutiny made into the claims of all who seek it—the prosperity for which all pray will come as soon, and be far more likely to stay when come it does."

Now, in the summer of 1875, the writer foreseeing a season of disaster, and being aware of the inability of the "Commercial Agencies" to keep their subscribers posted on the rapidly shifting financial condition of their customers, conceived a plan to assist merchants in exercising a better discrimination in selecting business risks. Although he met with very little encouragement at the time, he still thinks his plan worthy of adoption, and with this view is induced to give it to the public, in the hope that the next party who tries to engineer it will be more successful.

An office should be established in a location convenient to the business centers of a city, which should be placed under the charge of a skillful and rapid book-keeper. Books should be opened to contain the names of all parties who have become delinquent in their settlements, the information to be furnished by their creditors who subscribe to the enterprise. The subscribers should make up a list of their customers who are not promptly meeting their engagements, and who they have reason to suspect of weakness, together with the amount of each indebtedness. Every customer so reported should be assigned a separate page on the "General Delinquent Books" of the new office, and the name of each of his creditors, with the amount due should be entered thereon. Every morning, the subscribers should send to the office a list of payments (if any) made by delinquents already reported, together with the names and indebtedness of any new houses that have incurred their suspicion. Any information so received should be posted at once by the "General Delinquent Book-keeper" to the page to which it relates. A complete record can thus be kept of the entire amount of indebtedness of every person buying goods in the city. Now, when a subscriber receives an order from a party with whose standing he is not acquainted, he can send to the Delinquent Office for a list of the creditors of such party, and the information to be thus obtained would of course be much more reliable than what could be furnished by the Commercial Agencies.

The difficulties to be encountered in utilizing the plan, are:

First. A jealousy among merchants to disclose their business affairs.

A CHECK ON HAZARDOUS CREDITS. 63

Secoud. A reprehensible desire among merchants to have their neighbors sell goods to suspicious firms, in the hope that they may be paid from the proceeds of purchases made from a rival.

Third. The probability that if a delinquent is barred from buying goods in one city, he can buy in another.

These difficulties could be overcome by an energetic manager who thoroughly comprehended the situation himself, but it would require an immense amount of talking to convince some of our wholesale dealers that the plan was the best that could be adopted to protect them. The objections are answerable as follows:

First. For every disclosure you make of your own business, you may be recompensed by the disclosures of every concern in the city.

Second. For every risk you permit a neighbor to take, you incur the risk of selling to all the delinquents of all the other houses.

Third. It is not always possible for a buyer to change his source of getting supplies. If he has been in the habit of purchasing goods in one city, the merchants of another are pretty apt to know the reason for his desired change before giving him credit. They can get his general rating from the Commercial Agencies, and they would be inclined to scrutinize him more closely than they would if he had always traded with them.

64   SAFETY-BOOK-KEEPING.

If the idea met with the co-operation of merchants generally, the price of subscription to the "Delinquent Records" could be fixed as low as two or three dollars a week, and still leave a fair profit to the manager.

Accounting Books Published by Garland

NEW BOOKS

- *Altman, Edward I., *The Prediction of Corporate Bankruptcy: A Discriminant Analysis.*
    New York, 1988.

- Ashton, Robert H., ed. *The Evolution of Accounting Behavior Research: An Overview.*
    New York, 1984.

- Ashton, Robert H., ed. *Some Early Contributions to the Study of Audit Judgement.*
    New York, 1984.

- *Bodenhorn, Diran. *Economic Accounting.*
    New York, 1988.

---

* Included in the Garland series Foundations of Accounting
† Included in the Academy of Accounting Historians, Classics Series, Gary John Previt, ed.

■ *Bougen, Philip D. *Accounting and Industrial Relations: Some Historical Evidence on Their Interaction.*
New York, 1988.

■ Brief, Richard P., ed. *Corporate Financial Reporting and Analysis in the Early 1900s.*
New York, 1986.

■ Brief, Richard P., ed. *Depreciation and Capital Maintenance.*
New York, 1984.

■ Brief, Richard P., ed. *Estimating the Economic Rate of Return from Accounting Data.*
New York, 1986.

■ Brief, Richard P., ed. *Four Classics on the Theory of Double-Entry Bookkeeping.*
New York, 1982.

■ Chambers, R. J., and G. W. Dean, eds. *Chambers on Accounting.*
New York, 1986.
Volume I: Accounting, Management and Finance.
Volume II: Accounting Practice and Education.
Volume III: Accounting Theory and Research.
Volume IV: Price Variation Accounting.
Volume V: Continuously Contemporary Accounting.

■ *Clark, John B. (with a new introduction by Donald Dewey). *Capital and Its Earnings.*
New York, 1988.

- Clarke, F. L. *The Tangled Web of Price Variation Accounting: The Development of Ideas Underlying Professional Prescriptions in Six Countries.*
    New York, 1982.

- Coopers & Lybrand. *The Early History of Coopers & Lybrand.*
    New York, 1984.

- Craswell, Allen. *Audit Qualifications in Australia 1950 to 1979.*
    New York, 1986.

- Dean, G. W., and M. C. Wells, eds. *The Case for Continuously Contemporary Accounting.*
    New York, 1984.

- Dean, G. W. , and M. C. Wells, eds. *Forerunners of Realizable Values Accounting in Financial Reporting.*
    New York, 1982.

- Edey, Harold C. *Accounting Queries.*
    New York, 1982.

- Edwards, J. R., ed. *Legal Regulation of British Company Accounts 1836-1900.*
    New York, 1986.

- Edwards, J. R. ed. *Reporting Fixed Assets in Nineteenth-Century Company Accounts.*
    New York, 1986.

- Edwards, J. R., ed. *Studies of Company Records: 1830-1974.*
    New York, 1984.

■ Fabricant, Solomon. *Studies in Social and Private Accounting.*
   New York, 1982.

■ Gaffikin, Michael, and Michael Aitkin, eds. *The Development of Accounting Theory: Significant Contributors to Accounting Thought in the 20th Century.*
   New York, 1982.

■ Hawawini, Gabriel A., ed. *Bond Duration and Immunization: Early Developments and Recent Contributions.*
   New York, 1982.

■ Hawawini, Gabriel A., and Pierre A. Michel, eds. *European Equity Markets: Risk, Return, and Efficiency.*
   New York, 1984.

■ Hawawini, Gabriel A., and Pierre Michel. *Mandatory Financial Information and Capital Market Equilibrium in Belgium.*
   New York, 1986.

■ Hawkins, David F. *Corporate Financial Disclosure, 1900-1933: A Study of Management Inertia within a Rapidly Changing Environment.*
   New York, 1986.

■ *Hopwood, Anthony G. *Accounting from the Outside: The Collected Papers of Anthony G. Hopwood.*
   New York, 1988.

■ Johnson, H. Thomas. *A New Approach to Management Accounting History.*
   New York, 1986.

■ Kinney, William R., ed. *Fifty Years of Statistical Auditing.*
New York, 1986.

■ Klemstine, Charles E., and Michael W. Maher. *Management Accounting Research: A Review and Annotated Bibliography.*
New York, 1984.

■ *Langenderfer, Harold Q., and Grover L. Porter, eds. *Rational Accounting Concepts: The Writings of Willard Graham.*
New York, 1988.

■ *Lee, T. A., ed. *The Evolution of Audit Thought and Practice.*
New York, 1988.

■ Lee, T. A., ed. *A Scottish Contribution to Accounting History.*
New York, 1986.

■ Lee, T. A. *Towards a Theory and Practice of Cash Flow Accounting.*
New York, 1986.

■ Lee, T. A., ed. *Transactions of the Chartered Accountants Students' Societies of Edinburgh and Glasgow: A Selection of Writings, 1886-1958.*
New York, 1984.

■ *Loft, Anne. *Understanding Accounting in Its Social and Historical Context: The Case of Cost Accounting in Britain, 1914-1925.*
New York, 1988.

■ McKinnon, Jill L.. *The Historical Development and Operational Form of Corporate Reporting Regulation in Japan.*
New York, 1986.

■ *McMickle, Peter L., and Paul H. Jensen, eds. *The Auditor's Guide of 1869: A Review and Computer Enhancement of Recently Discovered Old Microfilm of America's First Book on Auditing by H. J. Mettenheimer.*
New York, 1988.

■ *McMickle, Peter L., and Paul H. Jensen, eds. *The Birth of American Accountancy: A Bibliographic Analysis of Works on Accounting Published in America through 1820.*
New York, 1988.

■ *Mepham, M.-J. *Accounting in Eighteenth-Century Scotland.*
New York, 1988.

■ *Mills, Patti A., trans. *The Legal Literature of Accounting: On Accounts by Diego del Castillo.*
New York, 1988.

■ *Murphy, George J. *The Evolution of Canadian Corporate Reporting Practices: 1900-1970.*
New York, 1988.

■ *Mumford, Michael J., ed. *Edward Stamp—Later Papers.*
New York, 1988.

■ Nobes, Christopher, ed. *The Development of Double Entry: Selected Essays.*
New York, 1984.

■ Nobes, Christopher. *Issues in International Accounting.*
  New York, 1986.

■ Parker, Lee D. *Developing Control Concepts in the 20th Century.*
  New York, 1986.

■ *Parker, Lee D., ed. *Financial Reporting to Employees: From Past to Present.*
  New York, 1988.

■ *Parker, Lee D., and O. Finley Graves, eds. *Methodology and Method in History: A Bibliography.*
  New York, 1988.

■ Parker, R. H. *Papers on Accounting History.*
  New York, 1984.

■ Previts, Gary John, and Alfred R. Roberts, eds. *Federal Securities Law and Accounting 1933-1970: Selected Addresses.*
  New York, 1986.

■ *Reid, Jean Margo, ed. *Law and Accounting: Nineteenth-Century American Legal Cases.*
  New York, 1988.

■ *Sheldahl, Terry K., ed. *Accounting Literature in the United States before Mitchell and Jones (1796): Contributions by Four English Writers, through American Editions, and Two Pioneer Local Authors.*
  New York, 1988.

■ Sheldahl, Terry K. *Beta Alpha Psi, from Alpha to Omega: Pursuing a Vision of Professional Education for Accountants, 1919-1945.*
New York, 1982.

■ Sheldahl, Terry K. *Beta Alpha Psi, from Omega to Zeta Omega: The Making of a Comprehensive Accounting Fraternity, 1946-1984.*
New York, 1986.

■ *Sheldahl, Terry K., ed. *Education for the Mercantile Countinghouse: Critical and Constructive Essays by Nine British Writers, 1716-1794.*
New York, 1988.

■ Solomons, David. *Collected Papers on Accounting and Accounting Education (in two volumes).*
New York, 1984.

■ Sprague, Charles F. *The General Principles of the Science of Accounts and the Accountancy of Investment.*
New York, 1984.

■ Stamp, Edward. *Edward Stamp—Later Papers.* See Michael J. Mumford.

■ Stamp, Edward. *Selected Papers on Accounting, Auditing, and Professional Problems.*
New York, 1984.

■ *Staubus, George J. *Activity Costing for Decisions: Cost Accounting in the Decision Usefulness Framework.*
New York, 1988.

- Storrar, Colin, ed. *The Accountant's Magazine—An Anthology.*
    New York, 1986.

- Tantral, Panadda. *Accounting Literature in Non-Accounting Journals: An Annotated Bibliography.*
    New York, 1984.

- *Vangermeersch, Richard G. *Alexander Hamilton Church: A Man of Ideas for All Seasons.*
    New York, 1988.

- Vangermeersch, Richard, ed. *The Contributions of Alexander Hamilton Church to Accounting and Management.*
    New York, 1986.

- Vangermeersch, Richard, ed. *Financial Accounting Milestones in the Annual Reports of the United States Steel Corporation—The First Seven Decades.*
    New York, 1986.

- *Walker, Stephen P. *The Society of Accountants in Edinburgh, 1854-1914: A Study of Recruitment to a New Profession.*
    New York, 1988.

- Whitmore, John. *Factory Accounts.*
    New York, 1984.

- *Whittred, Greg. *The Evolution of Consolidated Financial Reporting in Australia: An Evaluation of an Alternative Hypothesis.*
    New York, 1988.

■ Yamey, Basil S. *Further Essays on the History of Accounting.*
    New York, 1982.

■ Zeff, Stephen A., ed. *The Accounting Postulates and Principles Controversy of the 1960s.*
    New York, 1982.

■ Zeff, Stephen A., ed. *Accounting Principles Through the Years: The Views of Professional and Academic Leaders 1938-1954.*
    New York, 1982.

■ Zeff, Stephen A., and Maurice Moonitz, eds. *Sourcebook on Accounting Principles and Auditing Procedures: 1917-1953 (in two volumes).*
    New York, 1984.

■ *Zeff, Stephen a., ed. *The U. S. Accounting Profession in the 1890s and Early 1900s.*
    New York, 1988.

REPRINTED TITLES

- *American Institute of Accountants. *Accountants Index, 1920* (in two volumes).
    New York, 1921 (Garland reprint, 1988).

- American Institute of Accountants. *Fiftieth Anniversary Celebration.*
    Chicago, 1937 (Garland reprint, 1982).

- American Institute of Accountants. *Library Catalogue.*
    New York, 1919 (Garland reprint, 1982).

- Arthur Andersen Company. *The First Fifty Years 1913-1963.*
    Chicago, 1963 (Garland reprint, 1984).

- Bevis, Herman W. *Corporate Financial Reporting in a Competitive Economy.*
    New York, 1965 (Garland reprint, 1986).

- Bonini,. Charles P., Robert K. Jaedicke, and Harvey M. Wagner, eds. *Management Controls: New Directions in Basic Research.*
    New York, 1964 (Garland reprint, 1986).

- *The Book-Keeper and the American Counting Room.*
    New York, 1880-1884 (Garland reprint, 1988).

■ Bray, F. Sewell. *Four Essays in Accounting Theory.* London, 1953. *Bound with* Institute of Chartered Accountants in England and Wales and the National Institute of Economic and Social Research. *Some Accounting Terms and Concepts.*
    Cambridge, 1951 (Garland reprint, 1982).

■ Brown, R. Gene, and Kenneth S. Johnston. *Paciolo on Accounting.*
    New York, 1963 (Garland reprint, 1984).

■ Carey, John L., and William O. Doherty, eds. *Ethical Standards of the Accounting Profession.*
    New York, 1966 (Garland reprint, 1986).

■ Chambers, R. J. *Accounting in Disarray.*
    Melbourne, 1973 (Garland reprint, 1982).

■ Cooper, Ernest. *Fifty-seven years in an Accountant's Office. See* Sir Russell Kettle.

■ Couchman, Charles B. *The Balance-Sheet.*
    New York, 1924 (Garland reprint, 1982).

■ Couper, Charles Tennant. *Report of the Trial ... Against the Directors and Manager of the City of Glasgow Bank.*
    Edinburgh, 1879 (Garland reprint, 1984).

■ Cutforth, Arthur E. *Audits.*
    London, 1906 (Garland reprint, 1982).

■ Cutforth, Arthur E. *Methods of Amalgamation.*
    London, 1926 (Garland reprint, 1982).

- Deinzer, Harvey T. *Development of Accounting Thought.*
    New York, 1965 (Garland reprint, 1984).

- De Paula, F.R.M. *The Principles of Auditing.*
    London, 1915 (Garland reprint, 1984).

- Dickerson, R. W. *Accountants and the Law of Negligence.*
    Toronto, 1966 (Garland reprint, 1982).

- Dodson, James. *The Accountant, or, the Method of Bookkeeping Deduced from Clear Principles, and Illustrated by a Variety of Examples.*
    London, 1750 (Garland reprint, 1984).

- Dyer, S. *A Common Sense Method of Double Entry Bookkeeping, on First Principles, as Suggested by De Morgan. Part I, Theoretical.*
    London, 1897 (Garland reprint, 1984).

- *† Edwards, James Don. *History of Public Accounting in the United States.*
    East Lansing, 1960 (Garland reprint, 1988).

- *† Edwards, James Don, and Robert F. Salmonson. *Contributions of Four Accounting Pioneers: Kohler, Littleton, May, Paton.*
    East Lancing, 1961 (Garland reprint, 1988).

- *The Fifth International Congress on Accounting, 1938 [Kongress-Archiv 1938 des V. Internationalen Prüfungs- und Treuhand-Kongresses].*
    Berlin, 1938 (Garland reprint, 1986).

- Finney, A. H. *Consolidated Statements.*
    New York, 1922 (Garland reprint, 1982).

- Fisher, Irving. *The Rate of Interest.*
    New York, 1907 (Garland reprint, 1982).

- Florence, P. Sargant. *Economics of Fatigue and Unrest and the Efficiency of Labour in English and American Industry.*
    London, 1923 (Garland reprint, 1984).

- *Fourth International Congress on Accounting 1933.*
    London, 1933 (Garland reprint, 1982).

- Foye, Arthur B. *Haskins & Sells: Our First Seventy-Five Years.*
    New York, 1970 (Garland reprint, 1984).

- *† Garner, Paul S. *Evolution of Cost Accounting to 1925.*
    University, Alabama, 1925 (Garland reprint, 1988).

- Garnsey, Sir Gilbert. *Holding Companies and Their Published Accounts.* London, 1923. Bound with Sir Gilbert Garnsey. *Limitations of a Balance Sheet.*
    London, 1928 (Garland reprint, 1982).

- Garrett, A. A. *The History of the Society of Incorporated Accountants, 1885-1957.*
    Oxford, 1961 (Garland reprint, 1984).

- Gilman, Stephen. *Accounting Concepts of Profit.*
    New York, 1939 (Garland reprint, 1982).

■ Gordon, William. *The Universal Accountant, and Complete Merchant ...* [Volume II].
    Edinburgh, 1765 (Garland reprint, 1986).

■ Green, Wilmer. *History and Survey of Accountancy.*
    Brooklyn, 1930 (Garland reprint, 1986).

■ Hamilton, Robert. *An Introduction to Merchandise, Parts IV and V (Italian Bookkeeping and Practical Bookkeeping).*
    Edinburgh, 1788 (Garland reprint, 1982).

■ Hatton, Edward. *The Merchant's Magazine; or, Tradesman's Treasury.* London, 1695 (Garland reprint, 1982).
Hills, George S. *The Law of Accounting and Financial Statements.*
    Boston, 1957 (Garland reprint, 1982).

■ *A History of Cooper Brothers & Co. 1854 to 1954.*
    London, 1954 (Garland reprint, 1986).

■ Hofstede, Geert. *The Game of Budget Control.*
    Assen, 1967 (Garland reprint, 1984).

■ Howitt, Sir Harold. *The History of the Institute of Chartered Accountants in England and Wales 1880-1965, and of Its Founder Accountancy Bodies 1870-1880.*
    London, 1966 (Garland reprint, 1984).

■ Institute of Chartered Accountants in England and Wales and The National Institute of Social and Economic Research. *Some Accounting Terms and Concepts.* See F. Sewell Bray.

- Institute of Chartered Accountants of Scotland. *History of the Chartered Accountants of Scotland from the Earliest Times to 1954.*
    Edinburgh, 1954 (Garland reprint, 1984).

- *International Congress on Accounting 1929.*
    New York, 1930 (Garland reprint, 1982).

- Jaedicke, Robert K., Yuji Ijiri, and Oswald Nielsen, eds. *Research in Accounting Measurement.*
    American Accounting Association,
    1966 (Garland reprint, 1986).

- Keats, Charles. *Magnificent Masquerade.*
    New York, 1964 (Garland reprint, 1982).

- Kettle, Sir Russell. *Deloitte & Co. 1854-1956.* Oxford, 1958. *Bound with* Ernest Cooper. *Fifty-seven Years in an Accountant's Office.*
    London, 1921 (Garland reprint, 1982).

- Kitchen, J., and R. H. Parker. *Accounting Thought and Education: Six English Pioneers.*
    London, 1980 (Garland reprint, 1984).

- Lacey, Kenneth. *Profit Measurement and Price Changes.*
    London, 1952 (Garland reprint, 1982).

- Lee, Chauncey. *The American Accomptant.*
    Lansingburgh, 1797 (Garland reprint, 1982).

- Lee, T. A., and R. H. Parker. *The Evolution of Corporate Financial Reporting.*
    Middlesex, 1979 (Garland reprint, 1984).

- *† Littleton, A. C.. *Accounting Evolution to 1900.*
    New York, 1933 (Garland reprint, 1988).

- Malcolm, Alexander. *The Treatise of Book-Keeping, or, Merchants Accounts; In the Italian Method of Debtor and Creditor; Wherein the Fundamental Principles of That Curious and Approved Method Are Clearly and Fully Explained and Demonstrated ... To Which Are Added, Instructions for Gentlemen of Land Estates, and Their Stewards or Factors: With Directions Also for Retailers, and Other More Private Persons.*
    London, 1731 (Garland reprint, 1986).

- Meij, J. L., ed. *Depreciation and Replacement Policy.*
    Chicago, 1961 (Garland reprint, 1986).

- Newlove, George Hills. *Consolidated Balance Sheets.*
    New York, 1926 (Garland reprint, 1982).

- North, Roger. *The Gentleman Accomptant; or, An Essay to Unfold the Mystery of Accompts; By Way of Debtor and Creditor, Commonly Called Merchants Accompts, and Applying the Same to the Concerns of the Nobility and Gentry of England.*
    London 1714 (Garland reprint, 1986).

- *Proceedings of the Seventh International Congress of Accountants.* Amsterdam, 1957 (Garland reprint, 1988).

- Pryce-Jones, Janet E., and R. H. Parker. *Accounting in Scotland: A Historical Bibliography.*
    Edinburgh, 1976 (Garland reprint, 1984).

- *Reynolds, W. B., and F. W. Thornton. *Duties of a Junior Accountant* [three editions].
    New York, 1917, 1933, 1953
    (Garland reprint, 1988).

- Robinson, H. W. *A History of Accountants in Ireland.*
    Dublin, 1964 (Garland edition, 1984).

- Robson, T. B. *Consolidated and Other Group Accounts.*
    London, 1950 (Garland reprint, 1982).

- Rorem, C. Rufus. *Accounting Method.*
    Chicago, 1928 (Garland reprint, 1982).

- Saliers, Earl A., ed. *Accountants' Handbook.*
    New York, 1923 (Garland reprint, 1986).

- Samuel, Horace B. *Shareholder's Money.*
    London, 1933 (Garland reprint, 1982).

- *The Securitites and Exchange Commission in the Matter of McKesson & Robbins, Inc. Report on Investigation.*
    Washington, D. C., 1940 (Garland reprint, 1982).

- *The Securities and Exchange Commission in the Matter of McKesson & Robbins, Inc. Testimony of Expert Witnesses.*
    Washington, D. C., 1939 (Garland reprint, 1982).

- Shaplen, Roger. *Kreuger: Genius and Swindler.*
    New York, 1960 (Garland reprint, 1986).

- Singer, H. W. *Standardized Accountancy in Germany. (With a new appendix.)*
    Cambridge, 1943 (Garland reprint, 1982).

- *The Sixth International Congress on Accounting.*
    London, 1952 (Garland reprint, 1984).

- Stewart, Jas. C. (with a new introductory note by T. A. Lee). *Pioneers of a Profession: Chartered Accountants to 1879.*
    Edinburgh, 1977 (Garland reprint, 1986).

- Thompson, Wardbaugh. *The Accomptant's Oracle: or, a Key to Science, Being a Compleat Practical System of Book-keeping.*
    York, 1777 (Garland reprint, 1984).

- *Thornton, F. W. *Duties of the Senior Accountant.* New York, 1932. *Bound with.* John C. Martin. *Duties of Junior and Senior Accountants, Supplement of the CPA Handbook.*
    New York, 1953 (Garland reprint, 1988).

- Vatter, William J. *Managerial Accounting.*
    New York, 1950 (Garland reprint, 1986).

- Woolf, Arthur H. *A Short History of Accountants and Accountancy.*
    London, 1912 (Garland reprint, 1986).

- Yamey, B. S., H. C. Edey, and Hugh W. Thomson. *Accounting in England and Scotland: 1543-1800.*
    London, 1963 (Garland reprint, 1982).